Small Steps

Small Steps

BLESSINGS TO LIFT YOUR SOUL ON THE PILGRIMAGE OF LIFE

KIMBERLY KNOWLE-ZELLER

Morehouse Publishing
19 East 34th Street
New York, NY 10016
www.churchpublishing.org

Morehouse Publishing is an imprint of Church Publishing Incorporated.

Cover design by David Baldeosingh Rotstein
Typeset by Westchester Publishing Services

ISBN 978-1-64065-952-0 (paperback)
ISBN 978-1-64065-953-7 (eBook)

Library of Congress Control Number: 2026932996

For my mom, whose blessings always encouraged me to fly.

CONTENTS

SPIRITUAL JOURNEYS

GETTING LOST

RETURNING HOME

INTRODUCTION

Wear Your Boots

I don't remember the first time I received a blessing, nor when I first offered one myself. I only know that looking back, the giving and receiving of blessings have been with me from before I could even talk. Somewhere along the way, I came to understand that blessings can always be asked for and should never be withheld from being given to others.

Blessings are words we offer to share goodness and hope.

In the life of faith, blessings anchor ancient practices to our current lives. In my Lutheran tradition, at baptism, we hear the pastor say: *Stir up in this child the gift of your Holy Spirit: the spirit of wisdom and understanding, the spirit of counsel and might, the spirit of knowledge and the fear of the Lord, the spirit of joy in your presence, both now and forever.*

Following communion: *May the body and blood of our Lord Jesus Christ strengthen you and keep you in his peace.*

Before a sermon, the preacher offers a blessing: *May the words of my mouth and the meditation of my heart be acceptable to you, Lord.*

In our homes, we offer blessings for meals and transitions. *Come Lord Jesus, be our guest and let these gifts to us be blessed.*

We bless at bedtime for a peaceful night's rest, inviting the Lord to watch over us as we sleep and wake. We bless with words and also with our hands, by making the sign of the cross or placing our hands on shoulders.

Blessings are words that can comfort or convict, delight and surprise, renew and sustain. They are real words that meet real people in their real day-to-day lives. A blessing doesn't sugarcoat the truth to make it more palatable. Blessings have grit and grace, they know how beautiful and terrifying the world can be. But the blessing binds us together precisely so we can face the challenges ahead. So, we can link arms and walk hand in hand through heartache, loss, a diagnosis, changing relationships, or an unsettled heart. A blessing grabs your hands, looks you in the eyes, and says: *You are not alone.*

Two months after graduating from college, I flew to The Gambia, West Africa, as a Peace Corps Volunteer. This was 2004, and cell phone reception was spotty at best. The few opportunities to talk on the phone involved hours of walking and praying that any reception would hold out. The only realistic and reliable way to communicate with my family and friends was through letters.

For two years, letters became my lifeline. I scribbled prayers, updates, and thoughts about the newness I felt in my life on paper by candlelight while lying in bed under a mosquito net. Writing helped me make sense of my experiences: eating with my hands, bathing with a bucket of water, learning a local dialect, understanding the power of greeting everyone you meet, delving into the local school system, and learning more about the challenges children faced.

When the mail truck came monthly to my village, I often stayed inside my hut afterward for hours, poring over the replies from family and friends. Sitting inside my African home with the door open and a breeze to relieve the heat, I'd hear the women talking outside while I immersed myself in the words from home. I delighted in feeling close to friends through their unique handwriting. Two of my best friends from college were in Japan and India, and we all shared joys and challenges with one another, as well as the foods and comforts we missed from home.

My parents' letters came most frequently, and those were the ones I looked forward to the most. My mom told me of her day-to-day activities and life back home teaching special education at her local middle school. I heard about where she went to eat and what books she was reading. She kept me informed about our dog, a black lab named BJ. She always wrote, "I love you."

My dad also told me he loved me, and to be safe. He asked me to write back. He'd tell me how proud he was of me, and all the lessons I was learning. But he always signed off with the same refrain:

Remember to wear your boots.

Before I left for The Gambia, I did my due diligence researching the country and people. So did my parents. We learned hippos were prevalent in and along The Gambia River, which meandered through the entirety of the country. So was the poisonous Green Anaconda snake. My dad's words—*remember to wear your boots*—offered practical advice designed to keep me safe. He was worried for me. He was concerned for my health—for snake bites, cuts, infections, being so far away from a nurse, and for dangerous hippo attacks.

But those words were also something else: a blessing and a benediction.

My dad believed in my work as a Peace Corps Volunteer. He believed in cross-cultural learning and sharing, and stepping out of our comfort zones. He sent me with his blessing and approval, never once telling me to stay home and find a different job. No, he knew the risks, what the stakes were, yet sent me into the world anyway.

Remember to wear your boots was my dad's blessing for me, rooted in his belief in the God who binds us all together, from across oceans to across our city streets—the God who is always with us.

He also knew the realities of this world. The pain and brokenness. The violence and war. The failed relationships. The incurable sickness. The stress and weight of trying to make a living and following one's dreams.

This is the world he knew we are called to enter. This is the world we are called to be fully present in. To board a plane to a country and a people whom I had never heard of before, but to trust that I didn't go alone.

To wear boots was his reminder to me that the life ahead of us is hard and holy work.

Over time, I shifted from being a passive recipient of blessings to becoming an active giver—first as a pastor and then as a mother. I spoke the ancient words of blessing while leading worship and also began writing my own. Beside hospital beds, I blessed parishioners with words of healing and hope. Meeting a family and their baby, I blessed the gift of new life. When I became a parent, the prayers and blessings of others were sometimes all I had to give me strength. They sustained me during long nights and as I questioned everything from feeding to sleep schedules to missed milestones.

Every night, as they lie in bed, I make the sign of the cross over my children and remind them that they are loved by God. When I don't have any other words, and I'm exhausted from the day's tasks or feeling like I'm failing as a parent, marking the cross on their foreheads is an act of resistance for me. Resistance against feeling like my work doesn't matter. The sign of the cross reminds me of my call, both as a mother and as a beloved child of God. In blessing my children, I'm relying on a centuries-old tradition that conveys the power of God's presence, following in the footsteps of generations. Neither my children nor I are alone. The words become a way to share the gift of God's presence with myself and them.

The blessings ahead are meant to share God's presence with you, as they meet you in your real life. Your everyday, nitty-gritty, down-in-the-dirt, dishes-piled-in-the-sink, appointment-scheduling, carpool-waiting, caring-for-family-and-friends life. Your life as it is. In all the joys and challenges. In the moments when you'd rather stay inside, block out the news, and retreat with only your family. In the hours you spend putting one tired foot in front of the other.

The following blessings are divided into seven sections, based on the stages of pilgrimage. I am an avid walker, and one summer I spent a month hiking the Camino de Santiago in Northern Spain. The Camino is an ancient pilgrimage route that traverses France and Spain, with the destination of the cathedral in Santiago de Compostela. The Way leads through large cities, small hamlets, vineyards, and open fields. Over the course of 33 days and 480 miles, I encountered rain and fog, mud and pain, sunshine and beauty. I was met by the kindness of strangers as well as hours of solitude and stories from fellow pilgrims.

Pilgrimage is a lens through which I view the world, a lens that teaches me to keep going, in any circumstance. To move through the world paying attention and trusting that each step is an act of hope. *Small Steps* uses this lens—attention, hope, and faithful movement—and encourages readers to see the life before them as holy ground.

My hope is that you will feel these words wash over you and pour into your life. Then, that you will go and offer them to someone else. See the words multiply and scatter. Hear the hum of God's presence in every word: *You are not alone, you are not alone, you are not alone.*

For blessings aren't meant to be kept to ourselves.

In many churches, a final blessing is said to conclude the worship service. The words of this closing benediction are words I've said countless times as a pastor:

> *The Lord bless you and keep you.*
> *The Lord's face shine on you with grace and mercy.*
> *The Lord look upon you with favor and give you peace*
> (Numbers 6:24-26 NIV)

The final blessing sends people into the world. Never does the pastor encourage us to stay in the safety of the pews, but, rather, to face the world head on. With God's blessing. With God's presence. With God calling to each of us beloved children.

So, go out.

Pray.

Be blessed—and bless one another.

Love and serve. Take one step after another.

And remember to wear your boots.

YEARNING

A Desire to Walk

Serving as a Peace Corps Volunteer in Africa, I first learned of the Camino de Santiago.

Resting in a hammock one afternoon, I held Paulo Coelho's *The Pilgrimage* over my face as a shield from the sun and read the adventures of Coelho walking the Camino himself. I learned that the Camino is an ancient pilgrimage route that people have been traveling since the medieval ages. The legend goes that centuries ago, in a field in Spain, a religious hermit followed a star and found the bones of Jesus's apostle James. The bones were later confirmed by the bishop to belong to James and later, a cathedral was built on that spot. Since that time, pilgrims have flocked to Santiago de Compostela, along a route that became known as the Way of St. James.

I learned that people from across the world have longed to pray at the feet of St. James on behalf of themselves and their families. Many believed in the healing properties of the saint's bones. For every pilgrim, there are just as many reasons for embarking on the pilgrimage. During the Middle Ages, walking the Way of St. James was in and of itself a perilous proposition—walkers never knew if they would return home due to the threats of robbers, sickness, uncertain weather, and arduous passage through the mountains. Yet, they continued to walk and do so today with the hopes of reaching Santiago to pray and meet St. James.

Something stirred deep within me.

Suddenly, I saw hints of pilgrimage everywhere.

While I read Coelho's words, I recognized my life in The Gambia as a sort of pilgrimage, too, where I was also learning and immersing myself in a different culture. In Africa, my feet were my only reliable mode of transportation. Walking allowed me to experience both the fullness and simplicity of my life in Africa. I walked miles to visit neighboring communities and local markets, smelling fresh roasted peanuts, open fires, and green tea brewing as I went. My ears would perk up to hear the continuous pounding of coos and rice in wooden mortars and pestles. I walked to fetch my own water at the well and delighted in hearing the women talk and laugh while filling their buckets. I walked to help water small garden plots of red and yellow peppers. I walked to the local school with students. I walked to attend Friday prayers at the mosque. I walked past towering baobab trees and expansive rice and peanut fields. At night, the star-filled sky lit my way. Walking, the daily ritual of putting one foot in front of the other, connected me to both the land and its people.

After I finished *The Pilgrimage*, I began to imagine what it would be like to walk 500 miles across another foreign country. Excitement bubbled within me. I wondered what lessons I could unearth by walking day after day and with only the supplies I carried on my back. I wondered if I could connect to the land in Spain as deeply as I did in Africa.

After returning to the United States for seminary following my time in Africa, I met two others connected with the school who had walked the Camino. It felt like more than a coincidence. My heart kept thinking about this specific walk and what it could be like. Now back in urban America, walking as a necessity had ended. I missed putting my feet on the ground and walking to visit friends, to shop, and to see the beauty around me. I missed my life in Africa, but after hearing more about the Camino, I grew hopeful about what my future might hold, and I knew I needed to pay attention.

Have you ever had a similar experience—where you learn about something or someone and then you start seeing it everywhere? You learn a new word and suddenly others around you are using it in sentences. You notice a beautiful shade of green on your favorite car and then other cars driving by have that same color? Your child comes home with a new-to-them concept from science class and you hear about it everywhere, from the books you're reading to the posts you're scrolling past on social media?

This is known as the Baader-Meinhof phenomenon. Our brains are wired to notice. So, once a person learns something new, or notices a new thing, the brain is now able to recognize it more easily. Looking back, it doesn't feel like a coincidence that I first learned of the Camino while living overseas and feeling deeply connected to the earth through walking. God uses all those seemingly disparate occurrences and chance encounters to move in us, to help us see more deeply what God has known all along.

Those moments when you're brought to tears by a song on the radio, or a kind word from a friend, or the taste of homemade chocolate chip cookies—pay attention.

When you watch an acquaintance at their job and think, *I want to do what they're doing*—pay attention.

When you lose yourself for hours in a book, painting, knitting, or cooking from scratch—pay attention.

Call it what you will—Baader-Meinhof phenomenon, coincidence, luck—but I believe it's the Spirit at work in us, inviting us to see what we're capable of and how much we have to offer the world.

I did eventually walk my own pilgrimage on the Camino de Santiago. But I've learned that we don't have to travel across the world to live a pilgrim's life: a life rooted in paying attention, seeing the holy in the ordinary, slowing down, and finding community in unlikely places.

We can do it right where we are. A trip to the grocery store or coming forward for communion at church can be pilgrimages—if we're willing to pay attention.

The way we raise our children and show up in our school, at work and in our communities can be chances for pilgrimage. Walking with others in day-to-day life, to help them see how loved they are, can be a pilgrimage.

Our lives are ripe for seeing God at work.

In the blessings below, I pray you'll find words to meet your own yearnings and desires. May they help you take the first step in trusting that you walk not alone.

A Blessing for Taking the First Step

Find a path
in the woods
or the park down the street,
perhaps the main street of your town
or the bustling city
and then be still,
feel your feet
press into the ground,
attune yourself
to the pulse of the earth.
Just listen.

When you're ready
look up
and around.
Notice the way the breeze moves the leaves
then stare into the faces of people who pass.
Smell the aroma of earth and grass,
gaze at the variety of colors of plants, cars, and clothes.
Just watch.

Put one foot in front of the other
step after step connecting to the ground

hands free and eyes open.
Prepare yourself for a stumble or a
    stubbed toe,
possibly a broken heart
for you cannot know what's ahead
whether a detour that forces you in circles
or a dead end that brings you to your knees.
Just know it's okay to go slowly.

Take your time,
bring along some bandages
in case of cuts and bruises.
Let someone hold your hand
and guide you in a new direction.
Trust yourself
that you have all you need.
Take a rest,
enjoy a hearty meal,
come back another day.
Just don't give up.

What Is Prayer?

The sounds of children's voices
the warmth of hands touching
the newly sprouted crocuses reaching for the sky
the breeze rustling across trees
the light filtering through the clouds.

The longing to feel God's presence
and to sit with God's word
the hope for days to come
the peace of a lit candle
the silence of a deep breath.

The sizzling of veggies over the stove
a warm cup of tea
fresh-made muffins left at the door
sticky hands reaching for cookie dough
bread and wine, given and received.

A cry for help
a plea for relief
a song of joy
a shout of praise
a whisper: *are you there?*

Is this prayer?
This note
and words
tapping of keys across the screen
waiting and wondering.

Could it be
all of this and more?
Moving through life
embracing ourselves in love
and those we meet
and all the world
proclaiming God's love
and our worth found in God
as we are named a beloved child,
God's prayer
calling us good.

A Blessing for Listening

Sometimes we want to listen
but our lives are so loud,
with children demanding our attention

begging us for snacks and candy and trips to the
grocery store
needing to be shuttled to practices and rehearsals.
Sometimes our work keeps us tethered to phones and emails
sometimes our bodies are in pain
and we spend hours on hold and in waiting rooms.

Sometimes we try so hard to listen
we memorize scripture verses
and read Jesus's words in the Gospels.
We have the hymns of our youth on repeat
we pray and pray some more
we close our eyes and ask for a response
we lift our eyes to the sky
and wait to hear God speak.

Sometimes we forget to listen
we're so set on making our own way
following the path we have declared is best
checking off boxes to get to what's next
doing what those before us have always done
moving forward as if we are in charge of our lives.

Sometimes we just need to stop,
and let God meet us in our lives
our busy, full, loud, chaotic, and beautiful days.
Sometimes we need a reminder
that God loves this world and our place here.

This blessing is for those who are listening
to all the words, voices, and stories that bombard us daily.
This is for those who crave God's voice
who want to hear truth and goodness
who want to know and trust
that the path they're on is where they're meant to be.

Blessed are you who listens to the advice from friends
who reads all the websites and blogs
who searches late at night
listens to doctors, specialists, and teachers.
Blessed are you who are wondering what to do
and which way to turn.

Take a moment
place your hand on your chest
feel your heart
beat and beat and beat,
and trust that God resides deep within you,
trust the small voice that whispers just to you.

And when you don't know what to do
or where to go
or what comes next,
this blessing will find you
offering you the hope
to keep moving forward
making your way
with the One who has already
made a way before you.

A Blessing for Desiring Faith

This blessing is for the one
who knows all the hymns
who can quote scripture from memory
who remembers their Sunday school teachers and lessons
who joined youth group sleepovers and fundraisers
who prays *Come Lord Jesus* and *Our Father*

the one who knows the tenets of faith,
yet longs to feel the closeness of God
and often wonders where God is in the midst of it all.

This blessing invites you
to set aside the Bible (for now)
and all the lessons from your childhood
and take a moment
to trust it's okay
to simply *be*—in the presence of God.

Find a place
where you can lift your head up to the skies
settle your feet onto the ground,
breathe in and breathe out
just be
just be.

This blessing will wrap around you
whispering in your ear
that your desire for faith
is in itself a form of prayer.
So keep desiring
and keep coming back
to this spot
and your breath.

May this beginning
be a spark
to remember the One who first breathed life into you
who cradles the earth and everyone in it
who treasures each one
and claims you as beloved.

May this beginning bring you back
to the reminder
that our faith doesn't have to be fully understood
or always look identical to the way we learned,
but rather it can simply be lived and experienced
in taking one breath in and out
saying God's name
opening yourself to the Spirit's presence.

This blessing was there
at the beginning of your belief
in your first steps of faith
and will still be there, always, even until the end.

This Is How We'll Live with Hope

We'll get up, again
turn down the news
turn up the laughter
share the knock-knock jokes, the ones that have no punch line
but bring fits of giggles nonetheless.
We'll make beds and breakfast
pack lunches and feed the animals.
We'll make a casserole
and drop it with a note to a friend
Thinking of you.
We'll make tacos and buy chips and salsa
deliver them to the family with a new baby
Welcome to the world, sweet one.
We'll make phone calls and handwritten notes
delight in children's scribbles, a cascade of rainbows and hearts.
We'll open doors and windows
listen to birdsong

watch the cardinal perch on the evergreen bush
the bees and butterflies hunt for nectar,
nature gently reminding us that seasons come and go.
We'll plant flowers and scatter seeds
water the vegetables and pray for fruit.
We'll weed and till and weed some more
we won't give up on that tiny bean shoot
and marvel at the cucumber vine's tendrils
climbing the trellis.
We'll gorge ourselves on fresh tomatoes
bag them for neighbors
make homemade sauce
indulge in the goodness of summer.
With a resonant chorus of:
Thank you.
You're not alone.
Let me help.
We're in this together.
I love you.
We'll put one foot in front of the other
we'll cling to prayers as if our lives depended
  on them,
as if our hope for the world insisted on them.

This is how we'll live with hope.

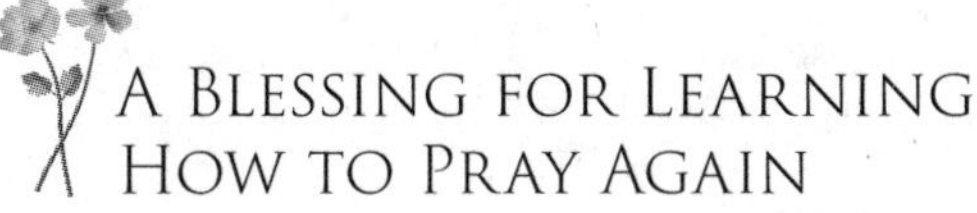

A Blessing for Learning How to Pray Again

If you desire
to pray
to talk to God like an old friend
to grow closer to the One who created everything,
if you wonder if God listens to you

or cares about the very real life you're living,
this blessing is for you.

Don't worry about the words
or how to say them
just be present to your breath.

Don't worry about what you look like
or how you hold your hands.
You can be standing or sitting
lying or walking
or waking to a new day
or ending it in bed,
just be present to your breath.

If you want to learn to pray again
go out into the world
place your feet on the grass
hold your hands open
say hello to anyone who passes.

If you want to learn to pray again
plant a garden and water it every day
marvel at the growing sprouts
keep throwing seeds to the ground.

If you want to learn to pray again
run around with your children
play hide-and-go-seek
read them a bedtime story
make up fairy tales together.

If you want to learn to pray again
say the names of countries facing war and unrest

look at the faces of those fleeing their homes
call your elected officials
speak out against injustice
and pick up litter along the street.

If you want to learn to pray again,
this blessing wants you to know
that *you* are God's prayer
sent to be grace and hope and love
for others
a prayer of love given to the world
and with every gift you share,
God draws near.

A Blessing for Going to the Water

If you need a reminder
of who you are
and whose you are,
go to a beach
and listen to the waves
lap over and over and over on the shore,
or go to a pond
or a lake.
Simply sit yourself beside some water
close your eyes and breathe the air
tip your face to the sky
extend your hands
and reach forward.

Feel the pull of the water
rock your body to its rhythm
trust you are held
and made of this water

that first formed this world
and pulses through your body,
water that nourishes and creates
renews and remakes
and lives inside of you
calling you home
to yourself,
wholly known
wholly beloved.

A Blessing for Never Saying Never

Never say never
to the big dream
the job that feels beyond your skill set
the reconciliation of a fractured friendship
freedom from aches and pain.

Never say never
to the hope for the future
when neighbors listen, even while disagreeing
and communities join forces for good
where democracy stands strong
and politics brings people together
across any divide.

Never say never
to receiving simple joys
a Hershey's Kiss
a child's handmade bouquet of wildflowers
someone complimenting your kindness
a few moments of deep breaths outside.

Never say never
because spring always comes again

the seeds in dark ground
burst forth to the surface
and people can change their opinions
and differences can be mended
addictions can be overcome.

Never say never
because God is always working in you
and calls you beloved
equips you
has placed dreams in you, ones to be realized
and walks with you wherever you go.

A Blessing for Dreaming

There's a dream inside of you,
waiting for the right time
to be set free in the world.

This dream is yours
your gifts and talents
the way you notice others
and bring out the best in them
it sees your hard work
the determination you bring and a heart that assures
others,
We've got this.

This dream has been building
one experience after another
through every trial and breakthrough
into long nights and early mornings
watching you sing songs of hope
and persevering
when everything else tells you to quit.

Now may be the time
to let this dream soar
(or it may need more time)
but trust that the dream of your heart
will not leave you.

So keep putting yourself out in the world
to learn and grow
to be stretched by fresh ideas
seeing new people and places
taking notes where your heart expands
and when tears come to your eyes,
this is your dream talking.

This dream
is yours for now,
but soon it will be set free
to bless and heal
to share love and joy
to bring peace to your corner of the world
and, in turn, to your heart.

A Blessing for Creativity in the New Year

Let this be the year
you notice the grip of your pen against
paper
the sound of keys bringing words to life
the softness of yarn stitching
the aroma of herbs mingling
the colors of paint against a backdrop.

Let this be the year
your eyes feast on light

your heart delights in the dance of leaves
your ears savor a chorus of laughter
your hands reach out to others.

Let this be the year
you find yourself
lost in beauty, ideas, and dreams.

And now
let this be the day
to carve space for you
to settle into stillness
to rest your heart
to offer prayers for peace
to allow your eyes to gaze on the gifts before you.

Let this be the hour
to dream
to write
to play
to connect
to create.

Let this be the moment
to begin.

A Blessing for Facing the Blank Page

When you come to the blank page
or blinking cursor
when the canvas before you
is waiting to be brought to life,
may you think in possibility
dreaming of what will come.

You may doubt what you have to offer,
but start writing anyway.

You may think you're not qualified enough,
put your stories down on paper.

You may worry about others
having already said what you want to say
or having said it better.

But don't hold back on releasing your creativity
for your words are the ones we need to hear.

Look in front of you at the page
and bring your whole self,
your memories
the secrets you've never shared
the prayers you release in the dark of night
and take this first step
one word at a time.

Start small with where you are
with what you love
and how you feel
what you see
how the light shines through the windows
the sound of the leaves rustling
the pitter-patter of footsteps down the hall.

Be only with the page
don't worry about others
and what they've written before
or what they'd say or think,
just trust yourself
and God's Word dwelling in you.

A Blessing for the One Longing for Deeper Friendships

This blessing is for the one longing
for deeper friendships
for connection and reciprocity
for friends who call and check in.

This blessing knows you try
it sees how often you text, call, and invite
and this blessing wants you to understand,
your friendship is a gift.

This blessing sees your yearning
to have a friend who knows you
and laughs with you, at all the same things
who picks up right where you left off
who remembers and connects.

This blessing knows you're trying
to be a friend and to make friends
and it sees how you question when to put yourself
 out there
or to be the one to go first.

This blessing is for the one who keeps showing up
with notes to encourage
invites for conversation
dinner with pizza and cookies on busy
 nights
and texts checking in:
How are you really?
Did you make that appointment?
How are the kids?
What can I pray for?

This blessing weaves a new story
one of expanding tables
that makes room for more faces and ideas
giving others a place to belong.

This blessing knows the power of forgiveness
and the gifts that come from honesty and vulnerability.

This blessing reminds you
that your desire is hard-won
and good,
this blessing whispers, *Keep going.*

A Blessing for When You Are Homesick

If the mention of home
smelling your favorite food
or catching a glimpse of the TV show you once watched as a family
makes you teary,
and if you're sad to see a group laughing while you're alone
and you can't figure out the mail system or public transport
or where to buy your groceries,
settle in and hear this blessing.

This blessing is for the homesick
the ones longing for a piece of the familiar,
the inside jokes
the ease of getting from here to there
your favorite meal
the warmth of your mother's hug.

This blessing is for those
learning a new way to live

within different languages or cultures,
the first year away at school or camp
even a new work environment
the one stepping out and away from all that is comfortable
and safe.

This blessing wants you to know you are brave.

While this is hard,
you have experience
you've tried and persevered,
so trust yourself
and lean on the kindness of others.

Take time to give thanks for all you miss:
friends and family
pets waiting for you
the cashier who knows your name
and a room of your own,
all reminders of how deeply loved
you are.

Turn then to the people and places
before you.
Notice what makes them come alive
and join them in their joy.
Ask lots of questions
marvel at learning some new skills
and don't be afraid to seek help.

Wherever you are
whoever you are with
they have been prepared for you
to help you learn and grow.

So, be inspired by your own courage
and, over time, find a new sense of your place
trusting that God is with you
wherever you are.

A Blessing for Saying No

When your heart knows the answer
but others are vying for your finite time and attention
volunteer organizations and church leaders see your gifts
want more of your talents and energy,
but you're feeling burnt out
like you don't have any more to give
and you need to refocus and be still,
may your *no* be clear and confident.

May your *no* lead to future opportunities
may it take away some worry
and leave trust.

May your *no* serve
as a firm foundation
one that moves you forward.

May your *no* be met with gratitude
for the work you've already done
and the smiles you've brought
the ideas that have rippled and multiplied.

May you not take on burdens
that were never yours to carry,
and when you release them
know that your time is valuable,
you are valuable

and with every *no* uttered
you offer a *yes* to yourself.

A Blessing for When It's Hard to Give Thanks

If the weight of the world
presses down on your shoulders
and the never-ending news cycle
brings you to your knees
if children crying out for help
consume your heart
if someone is missing from your table,
this blessing is for you.

If you can't find the words
or a smile won't form on your lips
if the days are a blur
feedings, diapers, and carpool lines
if you're lonely, tired, and exhausted
and the to-do's seem insurmountable,
this blessing is for you.

If you're wading through appointments and paperwork
swimming amidst the unknown
when doubts creep in and tears flow
when patience is thin and anger rises
and gratitude is the last item on your list,
this blessing is for you.

May you see a sunrise
or the sticky fingers of your toddler
the smile and giggles of your baby,
may you notice your kids' artwork on the wall and pause

may you be gifted a homemade pie
may a friend text: *I see you*
and your teenager say: *I love you, Mom.*

Maybe, just maybe, then
you summon a word of thanks
because this blessing wants you to know
many others share your struggle.

Remember, your story matters
and even a hint of gratitude expands
not only through your home, but across the world
in this moment and on this day
coming back to say: *you are safe, known, and loved.*

A Blessing for Unplugging

We're tired of the barrage of ways to be connected
of hearing our children ask for a tablet and a phone
of having our own devices, ever and always, in the soft palm of our hands.

And so this blessing resists the noise
the insistence on constant updates and info.

May we model for our children a life unplugged
may they see the fullness of life outside our screens
the power in looking up from our devices
and meeting the eyes of another human.

Help us to reclaim our time
to hold moments of in-person connection:
living room dance parties
building Legos

afternoons reading on the couch
picnics in the park
a walk across town
playdates with friends.

When everyone else has the latest and newest
keep us tethered to the natural world
devoid of screens but full of light
help us turn down the outside noise
and turn up the voices of those we love.

May we turn to those who share our
commitment
so we may not feel left behind,
but pave a way forward
hands free
and arms open
eyes alert and looking out
at this one beautiful
and priceless life.

May we see it all in vibrant colors
astonished by the brilliance of the real world.

A Blessing for Slowing Down

If you're feeling overwhelmed
if your mind is moving
in a thousand different directions
and you're unable to concentrate,
this blessing is for you.

If your body can't keep up with your mind
if your head aches and the days blend together

if you fail to take a break, even when you want to,
this blessing is for you.

If your mind wonders
and worries and frets
if your body is tense and tight
if your heart is tired of breaking,
this blessing is for you.

Be still.
Remember.
God is with you.

With every worry
hear God's voice
seeing you as treasured,
offering you a moment to exhale
to loosen your shoulders
hold your head high
not needing to prove anything
because you already are loved.

With every overscheduled moment
hear God's voice:
Come to me and rest.

Look up.
Breathe deep.
Be still.
Remember.
God is with you.

This blessing is with you
in the hustle and bustle.

This blessing embraces you
in the hurry
and holds you tight.

This blessing wants you to know
you, precious Child of God,
are enough
just as you are,
so rest
and be still
and remember,
God is with you.

A Blessing for Being Here Now

There's the unpredictable weather report for
tomorrow
no one knows if your son will make the team
or if your daughter will be left out by her friends
and if your aging parents will fall (again).

There's the replay of losing your patience
the exasperated sighs toward your children
the worry about what's for dinner
and when you'll eat between practices, games, and
schoolwork.

There's this, that, and everything under
the sun
or so it seems.

But really
there's only right now
and being where your feet are.

There's this moment
looking your loved ones directly in the eyes
listening to their voices
and noticing their bodies.
There's reaching out for a hug
and sitting down to kiss a scraped elbow.
There's enjoying the latest story of the day
and chopping the fruits and veggies for a snack.

There's right now,
breathing in and out
being held by the earth
cradled in love.

A Blessing for Paying Attention

May we be noticers
of moss growing on tree bark
the gentle wings of a robin
the way our partner gazes at us
the touch of our children's crumb-filled hand.

May we hear
the cadence of laughter
the delighted squeals of seeing snow for the first time
the hiss of the heater turning on
the tumble of wooden blocks.

May we touch
the soft homemade blanket across our lap
a sweaty hand in a high five
pen and paper writing a note of thanks
the worn pages of an adored book.

May we feel
the heartbeat of another next to our chest
the wind blowing through our hair
the welcome embrace when we return home
and a gentle kiss guiding us to sleep.

Keep our hearts open to the simplicity of the day
a day attentive to flesh, to faces, to reality
a day without the distractions of technology
a day seeing the people right in front of us.

A day of paying attention.

Help us, Lord
open our eyes
open our ears
open our hearts.

To know you are with us.

PREPARATION

Getting Ready for the Town Fair

Every September, our town of Cole Camp celebrates for three days during the Cole Camp Fair. When we first moved to our town, people told us, "Just wait, you'll love our fair." The town lights up for three nights with parades, rides, and all the burgers you can eat. The schools take a day and a half off for the fair. Kids and adults compete against one another in different games. Buildings throughout town display collections of locally grown produce, flowers, photography, hobbies, and baked goods. It's three days of celebrating the best of rural life. Three days of giving thanks for community.

On the Sunday before the fair begins, a parade of trucks makes its way downtown loaded with kitchen equipment and tools. A tractor follows, filled with long boards and A-frame structures. These trucks and the men inside make the first preparations by putting up the church's fair stand where the burgers, hot dogs, and pies will be sold. Members of the church have been coming to set up the stand for decades. Over the years, I watch elementary-aged children help their fathers hammer and pass out bolts, a legacy being handed down.

Sure, our town loves going to the fair, but we also love preparing for the fair. It takes months to get ready. There are fluffed-flower floats that need to be designed and assembled, requiring hours of fluffing and folding and attaching small paper-made flowers to cardboard. There is produce that has been grown and brought to be displayed, and cakes and desserts baked by the 4-H kids. The elementary art teacher arranges students' artwork. People assemble collections of Lego, sports cards, and jewelry for judging.

What I love about this time of year is the beauty of tradition and ritual. These are not the everyday rituals that come to mind when we think of the term. I'm talking about fluffing flowers for the parade floats, lifting up the roof on the fair stand, collecting produce to be on display, and the first bite of a hot cheeseburger fresh off the grill. These are the markers of our small-town life—and they remind me that life is richer when we work together and show up for one another.

Preparing for what's to come is as much a part of the journey as actually doing the thing. Whether preparing for a small-town fair or packing to leave on a vacation, there are lessons to be learned before every big endeavor. Before you can get on an airplane, you must pack your bag. Before walking the Camino, you must train through daily walks. Before a farmer can plant seeds, they must till the soil. Before spring can sprout into green, nature prepares for what's to come underneath the soil.

In the following blessings, may you remember the work that often goes unseen, or is less glamorous: the prayers you offer in the dark of night, the loads of laundry sorted and folded, the to-do lists. May you also see the importance of tending to your soul as you sip a cup of tea or close your eyes for rest. Through all the planning and preparation, God continues to prepare your heart, sinking into the deep soils of your dreams, forming you to be a bearer of love in all you do.

A Blessing for Beginning Again

You are here
not for the first time
but with the determination and experience
of knowing what it means to start anew.

You are here
with questions and doubts
and an eagerness to try again.

However you got to this point—
by sprinting or crawling
limping or smoothly
despairing or singing songs of joy,
this new beginning welcomes you.

To remember the people who walked with you
the places you've been
wins and celebrations
sleepless nights
moments where time stood still
missteps and hard-earned lessons.

This beginning invites you to see—
a rainbow prism of light glimmering on the floor
a child's bedhead and sleepy eyes
stick figures drawn on construction paper and flour-dusted
 counters
steaming hot chocolate from a mug
living room dance parties.

This beginning revels in the moments—
rocking your babies
shuttling to practices
calling a friend
helping with homework
reading books on the couch.

When you're here,
give thanks for your hands
for all they have held and carried
soothed and nurtured
for the food chopped
and the toys picked up
for backs massaged
for peace given with a single touch.

When you're here,
give thanks for your feet
for the games of hide-and-go-seek
the halls paced
the thresholds you've crossed.

This new beginning beckons
and invites you forward in hope
knowing the lives you've touched
and the lives you will continue to serve,
all with open hands and heart
daring you to dream.

A Blessing for a New Year

Come
pull up a chair
sit by the light

feel the ground beneath you
rest in the stillness of this moment.

Let this blessing meet you today
as you turn to a new year
and look back
remembering
reflecting
giving thanks.

Know this blessing
walked with you
in the early mornings and late nights
the nursing sessions and packing lunches
at the kitchen counter and the dining room table
the doctor's office and the school halls
playdates, family dinners, and walks
in filling out paperwork and waiting for answers
paying the bills
and working late-night shifts,
this blessing never left your side.

Know this blessing
found you in your scribbled notes
the paper, pen, and Google docs
the blank canvas
the thread and fabric
paint and paintbrush
the commute to work
the phone calls and spreadsheets.

This blessing
wove through your days
nestled in your fingers
warmed your heart.

This blessing saw it all
heard it all
felt it all
joy, grief, gratitude, awe, sadness, hope
and it's ready for whatever is to come.

This blessing is here
to make you feel
held in God's embrace,
and this blessing is here now
to tell you
you are enough.
It's looking you in the eye
grabbing your hands
and seeing you,
created in love.

Reasons to Wake Early

To bask in the quiet
startled by the morning light
a bath of pink, orange, and purple,
a new day full of possibility.

To listen to your breath
the stirrings of your heart
seeing to-dos as mysteries
to watch loved ones sleep
knowing they are safe and comforted
asking for that protective love to go with them all
their days
to read the words of others
to know you're not the only one
in the cries and tears and protests you offer
to write your own words and prayers.

May you keep coming back to this spot
this chair or your bed
this pen and paper
and feel supported by God's steadfast presence.

And on the days it feels impossible to get out of bed
or when the traumas of the world are too much to bear
or the pain too strong,
remember: Others are awake now
rising in the dark
praying for you.

A Blessing for Welcoming a Baby

You feel it with each kick and movement
your baby safe in your body's embrace
with every new pain and discomfort
swollen ankles and an achy back
your body is holding and caring for new life.
This blessing, like the baby safe in the womb,
is growing with you.

May you celebrate the strength of your body
because it nourishes you and your baby
because you carry the heartbeat of another
inside of you.

May you rest when you can
prop your legs up on a chair
breathe deeply
and trust your body.

If your child is coming to you
through adoption or foster care

may God give you patience
as you wait and wonder
and imagine the child who is waiting for you.

With every piece of baby clothing purchased or
handed down
may you see the threads of connection between family
and friends.
When putting together a car seat and stroller
may you dream of the places you'll go.
When tucking the crib sheet over the bed and shelving
baby books
may your baby's room always be a safe place.

When the time comes to welcome your baby into the world
may you be surrounded by gentle hands
compassionate providers
a community who prays
courage for the unexpected in labor
awe at the power of your body.

May the first sight of your baby
listening to the borning cry
mixed with your tears of joy
eye to eye
chest to chest
be one of homecoming
of love held and cradled in your arms.

May doubts be kept at bay
for you are the one chosen
to bring this baby into the world
following a long line of others
who have paved the way.

May your baby know now and forever
that they are covered in love
claimed by God
and making the world a better place
just by being here.

A Blessing for Putting on Your Shoes

Grab your shoes
the ones that fit your feet just right
with a little mud caked in the soles
scuff marks on the tip
and dust-covered laces.

Step out of your door
and into the world
and walk across dew-covered grass
stand tall, feet planted
letting the earth support you.

Do not take for granted
the gift of putting one foot in front of the
    other
keeping you mindful
of those for whom walking brings pain.

In every step, commit yourself to prayer
for the people you meet
the care of this planet
the path beneath you
those who have walked before you
and those who will still be coming.

May your mind slow
to the pace of your body.

May your shoe tread be strong
and the support unwavering
as your laces remain tied.

When walking through puddles and rain,
keep a light step.

When tripping on stones and climbing over rocks,
keep your eyes in front of you.

When walking uphill,
keep trusting in your strength.

When stumbling down,
keep getting up again.

When crossing city streets,
keep aware that everyone you meet is carrying something.

When passing farm fields and vineyards,
keep in mind that growth is everywhere.

When strolling neighborhood sidewalks,
keep praying for peace in communities.

When the horizon feels endless
may you put one foot in front of the other
for each step is a prayer
and an act of bravery
going forward with hope.

A Blessing for Working Out

We stand on our mats
arms reaching to the ceiling

rolling our shoulders back
circling our neck
working out kinks and soreness
stretching to prepare our bodies.

This blessing is for meeting you in your body
your wholly you and fully unique body
created and carved out by God,
loved just as it is.

This blessing knows the healing that comes
when you stretch and strengthen
breathe and increase your endurance
listening to your body
and honoring how it has supported you.

Bless these bodies as they begin
working muscles and gaining strength
bless our minds to push through any lack of motivation
bless our hands as we grip weights
and lift them up and down
one, two, three, four reps
and rest.

Give us a healthy relationship to our bodies
one that celebrates beauty and fortitude
that knows how much our bodies have held
how much has been stretched, changed, and aged
and how every fiber of our bodies is known by God.

Grant us determination to follow our own path
in taking small strides
as we learn new ways to care for ourselves
listening when we have pain
or have lifted too much weight.

May we not count the numbers on the scale
instead remembering the times we felt like giving up
but found ourselves on the mat
or running the trails
or picking the weight up for one more rep
showing up over and over again.

May we not compare the strength and stamina of others
but look at our own bodies
with their unique form and structures
how they've carried us through painful seasons
and give thanks for how God has designed us.

Commit us to seasons of rest
to looking at how far we've come
in strength, stamina, and perseverance
in looking at our bodies
and declaring them holy and good.

A Blessing for Researching

Grab a pen and notebook
request books from the library
turn on the computer
and give thanks for the access to information.

If you're planning a trip
or figuring out the best school and program to attend,
if a recent diagnosis has been handed to you,
if you're seeking input on the best education for your children,
or are looking for a new appliance,
this blessing is here to meet you
in the reading and researching
the seeking of knowledge and information
and finding the best way forward.

May you be sustained
through hours of searching
learning a new skill
or hearing firsthand accounts
seeking out experiences from others
and building a new vocabulary.

In every phone call or email
in the endless list of websites to scroll
may you find the information
that fits your family best.

During late-night Google sessions
when worry and impatience fuel your quest
remember that you are the expert on your life.

May you be discerning in what you read
looking to multiple sources
trusting that the people closest to you
can help provide answers.

And after you've exhausted all your resources
when you've read and studied
poured over the data
sifted through the reviews
called in experts and asked the mom down the street
highlighted and printed out statistics,
when it feels like you've come to the end of what you can know
and you don't know where else to turn,
look deep inside yourself
and listen to your heartbeat
listen to the life within you
and trust you have done all you can
and turn the next steps over to God.

A Blessing for a Rough Morning

Some mornings begin
when you're already done with the day
and don't want to get out of bed.
Each step takes too much effort
you want the blinds to stay shut
and keep out the hurts of the world.

If the thought of all there is to do paralyzes you
and you can't begin to fathom how anything will get done
and talking with people makes you nervous,
don't lose hope.

If you can't bear to hear another person call your name
with a request or task,
if the project was due weeks ago
and the bills need to be paid,
don't lose hope.

If you wake with a pit in your stomach
and can't stop replaying that one conversation
or hearing the news headline on repeat.
If the doctor puts you on hold again
and your child won't return the call
and it hurts to walk
and the fridge is empty,
don't lose hope.

The morning is here to greet you
gently and with love
like an old friend reaching out their hand
new mercies are rising
a fresh start is dawning.

A Blessing for Packing

Pull down a suitcase or backpack
check the weather and pick out your clothes.
Don't forget layers for cooler evenings
and a raincoat so you can keep dry.
Make sure you have enough toiletries and sunscreen
snacks for everyone to pass the time in the car or at the airport
a few books for reading and stuffies for comfort.

With every item you pack
may you say a prayer for safety,
and that your time away will be inspiring
full of new adventures,
that your time with family and friends will bring
laughter and moments gathered around the table
full of stories and reminiscing
and making new memories.

Remember that it's not only about what you bring
and what's stuffed in your bags,
but how you carry yourself
loaded with kindness
and compassion for your fellow travelers,
a smile on your face
extra patience for when plans go awry
or tempers flare.
Spread a dash of calm when the nights get late
and detours bring delays and altered plans.
Don't forget generosity
for yourself and the waiter,
the car that cut in front of you
and the family with the screaming baby.
Bless all these encounters

and may you be covered
in grace upon grace upon grace.

A Blessing for a Long Commute

Grab your travel mug,
an extra granola bar.
Make sure you have plenty of water
and your phone is charged.
Turn on your latest audiobook
or the newest dropped album
or relish the silence of being alone.
Take a deep breath
and say a prayer
for this blessing goes with you on your commute.

If your mind replays
the list of all you need to accomplish
if the messages and voicemails to return are long
if you don't know what's for dinner,
tune the worries and thoughts out
and listen to the engine's hum
the cars passing by.

See the other drivers on the road
picture each person as cherished by God
going about their day
with the hope of leaving their community better than before.
Every person holding stories and sickness and worry,
every person doing the best they can,
in need of grace.
This blessing invites you to pray for them
and the people they'll encounter
and all the lives they'll touch.

If your foot tends to press down hard on the accelerator
if you're quick to brake
take a pause and look before you
through the windshield and marvel at the road ahead
and all who have traveled its path.
Give thanks for the landscapes and waters
trees and parks
buildings and homes,
each piece a part of this vast world.

May you see this commuting time
as space with God
time to catch up and check in
conversing with God like an old friend
devoid of screens
or notifications pinging for your attention—
you are here
and so is God.

May your commute remind you of the privilege to work
providing for your family
and keep in mind those for whom work is a challenge.

In every stop sign
in every long stretch of highway
in the bumper-to-bumper traffic,
hold close to the One who is your safety
wherever you go.

A Blessing for Tending the Earth

Dirt falls through your fingers,
so settle on your knees
push a tiny seed into the ground

surround it in darkness
believe it will always lean toward the light,
and soak up water
and reach for the sun.

May all that lies underneath
bring forth fruit,
tiny shoots,
green sprigs
of hope.

A Blessing for Fall

We feel it, Lord,
the crisp winds, the hint of coolness
blowing through the air
welcoming a new season
a chance to start fresh.

We see the beginning of color—
red, orange, yellow
flooding our eyes and senses
reminding us of what is to come,
vibrant colors falling to the ground
welcoming a time of rest
quiet and darkness
where something will be growing
and building within creation
and in our souls.

As the seasons change
keep us open for your
Spirit at work
in an abundant harvest

a gentle rain
the chatter of creatures,
children's voices.

Teach us to notice
the needs of others
the cries of injustice
the stirring of our hearts.

Walk with us toward
healing for the sick
rest for the tired
peace for the anxious.

Hear our prayers
this autumn day
full of hope and promise
on the cusp of change
with the shortening days
reminding us
of Your light
that never fades.

A Blessing for Winter

God of the smallest molecule and the largest
galaxy
bless this winter season,
for the chill of the air
the smell of pine trees
and the stars' light dotting the sky.

Bless us this season
as we settle into waiting and resting.

Winter can feel so long and cold
layered in sweaters and coats
hats covering heads with eyes peering out
mittens for protection from frostbite
while shoveling driveways, scraping windshields,
and forming snowballs.

Sustain us this winter
when the days grow shorter and darker
as we wrap ourselves in the warmth
of hand-knit blankets and hand-me-down shirts,
keep us mindful of those who long for shelter.

Winter can also show great beauty
light reflecting on freshly fallen snow
icicles dancing and shining,
a sunset with barren branches scattered across the horizon
crisp blue skies
evergreens standing tall.

Winter has much to teach us
in resting and looking inside ourselves for reserves of strength
in creating welcoming places to come in from the cold
in celebrating small moments where the light breaks in.

May we light candles
training our eyes to follow the dance of the spark
believing that nothing is out of God's reach
compel us to not turn away from the darkness
but to meet it with tenderness
listening for what grows underneath,
trusting that beneath the layers of cold and snow
new life—seeds of hope—are being nurtured.

A Blessing for the First Warm Days

The snow piles are melting
glistening throughout the ground.
Layers of sweaters and coats, hats and gloves
have been stripped off,
oh, the glorious sun and blue skies.

There's a wisp of clouds,
the hope of all that's waiting beneath the surface.

May this thawing seep into our bodies
may we look into the eyes of our neighbors
with a wave and a good morning.
May we reach out to friends and offer: *I'm here for you.*
May any barriers and disagreements fall from us
and be filled with listening and understanding
sentiments of mutuality.

May the reality of what is
not be greater than the potential for what could be.

And may we be the ones unearthing this hope,
together and in community
for the sake of the world.

A Blessing for Spring

Give us moments untethered
hands free and eyes open.
Give us a gentle breeze
and the melody of wind chimes.
Give us robins hopping with worms in their mouths
and the flurry of squirrels chasing one another up and down trees.

Give us redbuds and daffodils
and the scent of lilacs.
Give us dog walkers and kids on scooters.
Give us city workers caring for the park
and children pumping their legs on a swing.
Give us deep breaths
and feeling held by the earth.
Give us the peace to trust nature's timing
and to know spring always comes again.

A Blessing for the Month of May

May we feel the power of new life springing from the ground.
May we sing a song of creation's glory.
May we trust that the sun will continue to shine.

Help us to remember
that in this month of transitions,
there is something new emerging.

Teach us to see the days as gifts waiting for us.

Teach us to savor the wind on our faces,
the smell of fresh flowers
the feeling of dirt in our hands
and the flight of the hummingbird.

May we smell the sweetness before us
jasmine and cherry blossoms,
and listen to the buzz of earth's heartbeat
hearing the frog's croak and the owl's call,
may we know the gentle touch of friends,
revel in the laughter of children,
and open our eyes to the blazing beauty before us.

A Blessing for Summer

May the God of the sunning turtle, calves and foals,
garden veggies and shade trees,
be with you this summer.

May you open your eyes
to the beauty in your front yard
a cardinal bathing
the shades of green leaves
the vibrant flowers.

May you open your eyes to the cadence of friends talking
children chasing one another through the grass
hands waving hello.

May your feet be firmly planted
reveling in the earth's support
reverent of your place in the expansive universe
cautious of your footprint on creation.

Open your hands
to strawberry-filled fingers reaching for a hug
one more push on the swing
another walk around the park.

Open your ears
to the convictions of fellow residents
the man asking for food assistance
the children who have one more thing to tell you.

Keep your Spirit set on seeking God
choosing joy over sadness
intent on singing a song of peace.

May the God of the gentle wind and rushing storms
trickling creeks and towering mountains
quiet your soul.

May you dig deeper
into God's Word.

With every daybreak and nightfall
may your body be a prayer
your life given in love,
for the sake of your neighbor
for the sake of the world.

A Blessing for the Garden

The wind moves through the grass
the mourning doves and wrens welcome the day with their
songs
and the garden waits in anticipation.

Before the first seed that is planted
before the water drenches the soil
before the sprouts burst through the ground
before flowers and fruit,
the garden waits in anticipation.

Your creation, Lord, is a gift
help us to honor this earth
and the animals and creatures that make their home here.
Help us to see Your presence in the tiniest seed
help us to give thanks for Your bounty with every turning
of soil
help us to wait and wonder
for the new life that is to come.

Teach us patience, Lord,
as the water nourishes the ground
as the roots take hold in the darkness.

And as the garden grows,
may our hearts grow too
in newness and hope
beauty and joy
praise and glory to you.

A Blessing for Nighttime

As our day winds down,
quiet our minds and our hearts
bring our breathing to beat in tune with Your heart, God.

With heavy eyes and a grateful spirit
help us to look back on the day
and see the love shared,
but also the missteps
when we said unkind words
or failed to listen to a friend
when our patience was frayed,
in all our moments
give us Your peace.

May we know love and when we have given it freely
may we sleep covered in blessings:
of conversation and meals shared
watching the clouds dance across the sky
an unexpected call from a friend.

Guard our hearts from worry
and when the bad dreams do come
help us to remember we do not face them alone.

Help our bodies rest
help our minds rest
help our souls rest.

May we learn to walk
more in step with you, Lord,
every day.

A Blessing to Welcome Rest

Blessed are we who seek your rest, Lord,
for our hearts are worn to a frazzle
from seeing unrest
and division across our world and country.
Our bodies are tired
from endless errands
and work demands and caring for our children.

We need you, Lord. Be our rest.

Can you hear the exasperation in our voices?
Do you feel the deep breaths taken to keep our patience intact?
Do you see us in our cars going from here to there and back again?
Can you count the open tabs on our computer browsers?
Do you feel the aches in our bones from standing at the counter prepping dinner and washing dishes?
Do you see us glance toward the bed, a pile of laundry still to be folded?
Do you see the number of times we're cleaning noses, diapers, and spills?
Can you count the Cheerios on the floor and stuck in couch cushions?
Do you know how many meetings we've scheduled and how many times we crave to say *no*?

Can you see the emails accruing one after another?
Do you see the hours lost mindlessly scrolling?
Do you understand our worry for the days ahead?

God, in these moments of unrest, keep us coming back
to you.

Help us to hear You calling,
Come and rest.
Teach us to recognize Your voice calling us,
You are my beloved.

Help us to stop and listen,
if only for a moment,
to feel the wind on our face
to hear the rustle of leaves
to smell freshly cut grass
to see the clouds beginning to break.

Your presence is with us
never having left
always there
always calling us back
and issuing the same refrain:

You are loved, you are loved, you are loved.
You are enough, you are enough, you are enough.
Come and know I am with you, always.

DAILY ADVENTURES

Stepping Off from the Front Porch

The front porch draws my attention first. Walking to the front door, the metal railing tilts to the side and shakes in my hands as I pull myself upward toward the door. I think about the many hands that have held this railing, seeking hospitality. I now add my hand to this history.

Next I notice the four maple trees. They stand tall and welcome me into what will be my home. I picture their vibrant fall colors to come. I'm mesmerized that these trees, this property, and this house are the first my husband, Stephen, and I will call our own.

We are newly married with no kids yet. Stephen is the pastor at the church across the street, and part of his call includes living in the church parsonage.

From the porch we look out to the town playground with yellow slides and cement tunnels. We quickly learn that at all hours of the day, children's laughter and shouts float to our home. The shelter houses parties and picnics. We put chairs outside so we can sit and wave to people passing by. The early mornings on the porch provide a refuge to me as I begin the day with quiet reading and writing. It's this porch that watches us grow as a family and welcome friends.

So it's fitting that the day Stephen and I bring home our rescue dog, Lars, we snap a picture on our front porch. The dog is young and healthy, and so are we. The picture represents us in all our newness, together in our first home.

I decide to take a picture on this day every year from now on as a way to chronicle the story of us, the story of our family.

Each year around our dog's Gotcha Day, we find someone to take our picture. The second year, I'm wearing maternity clothes, and by the third year, our daughter Charlotte is almost ten months old. In the fourth year, my husband has grown a beard. In the picture taken one month after my son Isaac was born, my eyes are barely open from squinting in the sun, and you can tell we're all a bit sleep deprived. As the kids grow, there's less room for the dog, and we all have to squeeze together on the porch steps.

Each year, I'm reminded of how much these steps have witnessed. For the past twelve years, this porch has seen our coming, going, and growing. This porch has held us and welcomed us. It's been a source of refuge and strength. It's provided a place to land through busy seasons and quiet afternoons. It's been transformed with hanging baskets in the spring and red ribbons for Christmas. It's been the gathering spot for trick-or-treaters, carolers, and neighbors dropping off fresh produce.

On this porch, we've opened the door to friends and family. We've looked out to witness the seasons changing. We've carried our children as newborns through the door and posed them for pictures on the first day of school. We've watched ruby-throated hummingbirds feed, children play at the park, and school buses drive by.

We've loved. We've laughed. We've cried. We've rejoiced on this porch.

We've become a family here.

Every year, as we arrange to take this picture, it feels like a pilgrimage to wrangle our kids, get the dog to sit and face the right way, and now make sure the cat doesn't jump out of our hands. Luckily, with the photos, we have a tangible reminder of how we've grown. But it's also about how much we've changed on the inside, too—growing in patience and understanding toward one another, deepening our resilience when plans change, and giving and receiving forgiveness.

We don't have to travel to new places, board a plane, or walk for miles on end to make meaningful connections. The daily adventures and the mundane routines of our days provide ample opportunities for deepening relationships, slowing down, and paying attention to the beauty around us.

For my family, the front porch is a place of significant meaning and where we've marked the changing seasons and growth among us by simply stepping outside our front door. As you read the following blessings, I hope you see the beauty and holiness in the life you're living right now. I pray you have moments to pause and delight in a walk in your neighborhood, or sitting in the school pickup line. I hope you can relish reading with your children and waking to a new day.

May you see your life as a pilgrimage, right where your feet are.

The Work of Our Hands

Bless these hands
in all that they do
and all that they carry,
these hands—
reach
embrace
fix
clean
cook

drive
push
create
paint
hug
hold
feed
write
color
bless.

Bless these hands—
the hands that grasp the One
who first reached out to us
declaring all of creation
good and holy,
a work of art.

A Blessing to Start the Week

God of minutes and hours
God in and above time
God the maker of time
and the essence that flows through all our days,
quiet our hearts and soothe our spirits
so we can rest and be present
to this moment and this new start.

May we see the moments before us
as doorways to Your presence.

Help us to step through each encounter
with openness and love
knowing your Spirit will not take us
anywhere you have not already been.

May we not rush our days
or waste time idly on our phones.

Keep a spirit of flexibility before us
for when interruptions come:
a call from school or work
sickness
a broken fridge.
Help us to lean into what we can learn
even when plans fall apart.

With every person
every moment
every misstep
every experience,
You are with us, God.

A Blessing for Monday

Monday
you are the slow start
to a new week
holding memories of waffles for breakfast
and rounds of Uno at the dining room table.

Monday
you are the invitation
to cross off the to-do's
make the appointment
get the lunches packed
and book bags stuffed with signed notes and library returns.

On Monday
the busses pass by
we step outside to the pink of daybreak

hot coffee steams from a chipped mug
the week stretches ahead,
but right now, Monday,
you unfold before us
full of possibility
one moment in time
to remember life keeps on
giving chances to start over.

A Blessing for Filling Out a Calendar

Before the turn of a new month,
take a moment to pause.

Before filling the days with practices, meetings, and rehearsals,
take a moment's rest.

Illuminate in us a posture of gratitude
as we look back on the days
where we've had challenges and joy
busyness and rest,
and help us to give thanks for God's presence.

As we turn to a new month
equip us to go forward with kindness
for ourselves and others,
kindness to our future selves for not filling the days too full.
Guide us as we go about our days
with meetings, grocery runs, and meal planning
as we write down practices, concerts, and games,
help us to pray for health and all who we'll meet.

Help us to not only see squares on the calendar
but love shared

gifts offered
prayers spoken
skills sharpened
friendship deepened
burdens lifted
and time with the ones we love.

In each day
sustain us as changes happen
the unexpected occurs
love deepens.

Through it all
when the day comes to an end
keep us mindful of where we've offered grace
extended forgiveness
and cultivated God's kingdom here on earth.

A Blessing for Seeing What's Before You

Look! A new day begins,
the dawn announced in shades of pink and orange
the morning light streaming through windows
falling across the walls
dancing with shadows.

Look! At the American goldfinch flying,
their songs greeting the morning
your loved ones covered in blankets
the cat stretching at the foot of the bed.

Look! In the eyes of your family,
listen to their stories
reminiscing about that time

grandma knitted everyone matching sweaters
and your parents drove through the night to surprise family for Christmas
and the drawings your youngest sibling did on the living room wall.

Look! Into the eyes of friends,
talk about the weather,
but also favorite books
and the challenging coworker
and the woodworking hobby they started.

Look!
See with the eyes of God
gazing at this creation
brimming with hope and love.

A Blessing for Walking in Your Neighborhood

Bless our two feet that walk
along city streets
one step after another
through side alleys
along country roads
keeping watch for uneven sidewalks
wondering about the lives of those behind front doors,
noticing flowers breaking through the cracks
stopping to wave to the retired man on his porch
and saying hello to the mother pushing a stroller.

Bless those who walk
with too-tight shoes and achy knees
with a limp or a skip in their step,

lathered in sunscreen and holding a walking
stick
listening to music or an audiobook.

May our senses be awakened,
to the wind on our face
the crickets' chirp
a car's horn
a woman's perfume
barking dogs
chimney smoke
a child's laugh
the hum of the earth under our feet
the richness of life.

Bless the feet that take us into community
to love as best we can,
seeing the world for how it is,
grabbing ahold of goodness at every turn
and believing
together,
we can walk toward
a new world.

A Blessing for an Ordinary Tuesday

In our rising,
help us to see You.

In our waking,
help us to feel You.

In our movement,
help us to trust You.

Fill our days with love,
a call from a friend
the dog sitting at our feet while we send emails
a positive note from a child's teacher
the cashier at the grocery store greeting us by name.

Today is another day,
but nothing is ever ordinary with You—
Your mercy shines in the beauty found in the golden hour,
the ripening of a fresh tomato, the splash of ocean water.
God's heartbeat can be heard in children's laughter,
the wind through the window,
the toll of a bell.

Today, may we be open to what lies ahead—
Your presence with us
blessing us
showering us with mercy
redeeming and renewing us
today and always.

A Blessing for School Supplies

God of ringing bells and classroom halls,
bless our children as we send them into the world.

Breathe your Spirit into this school year,
may it be filled with lessons and play
friendship and forgiveness
questions, challenges, and growth.

Be with us as we entrust our children to others
and open our hearts to the unknown.
We hope and believe in Your goodness

that Your love will meet us throughout our days
and be a beacon of grace.

We bless teachers and students
schools and families,
but also the supplies needed to do Your work in the world.

Bless pencils to write words of hope and love
bless erasers as they remind us what it is to forgive and be
    forgiven
bless papers and notebooks to be filled with stories, dreams,
    and unlimited potential
bless lunch boxes and water bottles to nourish and sustain,
    to give energy and life
bless earbuds and headphones so we may tune in to Your voice
bless markers and crayons to bring beauty and creativity to
    the world.

In the end, bless not only these items,
but the hands that hold them
the bodies that carry them
and the children whose hearts and minds will be shaped.

A Blessing for the School Pick-Up Line

Blessed are the ones waiting
for the first glimpse of their child
smiles that meet them across the parking lot,
your child seeing you and knowing
that you always come back.

This blessing is with you as you wait
amid a line of cars
with music and audiobooks

catching up on texts and emails
passing snacks to younger kids in the back seat
making one more call.

May you take a moment and a deep breath
a silent prayer for your child
their friends
and those who have surrounded them all day.

May your children know safety and love
their minds full of new facts and stories
learning about the world
and practicing kindness.

May you know your love has been bound to them
tethering them in the comfort of being known.

Bless the parents and grandparents,
the ones missing work to wait in the pick-up line
and the ones longing for their kids.

Bless the students,
the ones who are new
and the ones who are looking for a friend.

Bless the teachers,
who stand in the wind and rain, cold and heat
who know everyone by name
who worry about those who might not have enough food.

Bless the first moment of hello
the piling of backpacks in the car
a flurry of information from the day
chatter and laughter

I'm hungry
Can we go to the park?
What's for dinner?
Guess what I learned?
sounds of homecoming and connection,
a blessing to have a safe space to land.

A Blessing for Meal Planning

Another day
another meal to plan
the never-ending tasks
scouring through stacks of cookbooks
scrolling online
to plan
prep
cook
serve
and clean up.

Breathe inspiration into our meal planning
as we flip through recipes.

May we remember the people who will be fed
the conversations shared over plates of spaghetti
the prayers offered while passing bowls of green
beans
and the love shared with each bite.

Though the task of planning
and checking the pantry
and making shopping lists
feels tedious and sometimes thankless,
help us to see the beauty in feeding our family

knowing that when we gather at the table
we are nourished in mind, body, and spirit.

In the rush of busy weeknights,
may we not feel the pressure to cook from scratch
for fed is the goal.
Relieve any guilt when fast food becomes the default meal
or cereal again for dinner.

Help us to ask for help when needed
accepting a meal dropped on our porch
gift cards from friends
inviting our partner to plan a meal
and letting the kids take responsibility for their favorite foods.

When the time comes again to plan,
and we're tired and out of ideas
the cabinets are low on food,
sustain us with the One
who feeds us unending grace.

A Blessing for Welcoming a Guest

This blessing is here to tell you to extend the invite
when you're in need of community
and friends to sit across from you
who will hear your burdens
and hold your prayers
and your desire to know others more deeply.

For in welcoming guests,
we welcome God
to pull up a chair
and join us in the breaking of bread

and sharing of stories
in laughter and tears.

There is no perfect time,
for the dog hair will always be present
the bathroom will have smudges on the mirror
a child's sock and cleats will be strewn on the floor
the recipe will never be perfected.

Send the text
write the invitation
place the call
and open your door to welcome guests.

When your doors are open and your tables extended,
bless the conversation
sharing highs and lows
stories of pain and heartache
worry for your aging parents
fatigue at the state of the country
and the hope for finding common ground.

When the plates are full and the snacks are passed around,
bless the food that is handmade and took hours of
  preparation
as well as the delivered pizza and store-bought salad
the candy bowl the kids keep grabbing from
iced tea and lemonade
homemade cookies.

When the couch is full and extra chairs are added to the table,
bless the friends who help themselves to the kitchen cabinets
and start chopping the veggies for the salad
the ones who stop by the store for that needed spice

and the kids who run right to the playroom sharing toys
and learning young, that life is best lived in community.

This blessing knows that every time
you welcome someone into your home
you get the chance to show them
how valued and known they are.

This blessing binds together hosts and guests,
both with gifts to share.

May you be inspired to keep inviting
to prepare a longer table
and open spaces
to sit on couches with no phones
to pass endless bowls of chips,
and in every person who walks through your doors
may you see the face of Christ.

A Blessing for the Gift of Water

Bless the water that pours forth
from oceans and rivers
lakes and streams
nurturing and sustaining life,
home to creatures great and small
algae and mollusks
seahorses, dolphins, and whales,
the water pulled by the moon
that splashes onto shores and riverbeds,
where kids jump in waves
and search for shells
where crawdads and snails are treasures to be found
and the sound of a rippling stream calms a racing mind.

Bless the water that falls from the sky
gentle showers and mighty rains
water that supports plants and crops
seeping into the roots of community gardens
and acres of orchards
ripening tomatoes and peppers
bringing forth colorful blooms of zinnias and
sunflowers
and watering large crops of corn and soybeans,
water that pools on city streets
perfect for little feet to jump in
and the sparrow taking an afternoon bath,
the tap, tap, tapping of water
keeping in tune with our heartbeat.

Bless the water we drink
that quenches thirst
and relieves parched bodies,
water from fountains
and streams that we cup in our hands
filled in sticker-covered water bottles
passed out at marathons and parade routes
left on the side of the road for the traveler
the joy at the first sip on a hot summer day.

Bless the water used to cook and clean
to pour into pots and pans
simmering veggies and cooking meats
water that transforms into soups
and water to make lemonade and tea for guests,
bless the water that washes away dirt
and removes stains
soapy water we plunge our hands in for cleaning dishes
and water to rinse our bodies after a long day.

Bless the water that is within us
transporting nutrients and oxygen
protecting our organs and tissues
connecting us to earth
and every living thing.

Bless the water
this life-giving
life-sustaining
freely given gift.

A Blessing for Baseball

You pack your gear
lace your cleats
sling the backpack over your shoulders
and walk toward the field.

With every toss and catch,
as you run across the outfield
and in every swing,
keep your head held high.

Say thank you to the coaches
who offer their time and skills.

Cheer for your teammates
for the team is made of "we."

This is where you learn to work together
to keep chasing the ball
to get up when you fall
to lose with grace.

May the hours on the field
teach you the power of being on a team,
of encouraging your teammates
growing and stretching
trying something new
feeling the arms around you in a huddle
and the power in hands on top of one another
chanting *three, two, one*
play ball!

A Blessing for the Sidelines

When you find yourself on the sidelines
in the auditorium chairs
atop the bleachers
or working the concession stand,
may this blessing meet you.

May your voice bring encouragement
joining with others
seeing all players as a unified team
cheering for all as if they were yours
You got this!
Way to be a team!
We're here for you!

May you look up
and meet the eyes of fellow parents
recognize the players as kids wanting to
have fun
give thanks for coaches and referees sharing their time and
experience
and delight in siblings making new friends.

May you use your voice to uplift
to celebrate differences
and build up a group where all are welcome
with their unique gifts and strengths
believing that a team includes everyone.

Bless those who show up on the sidelines
with extra snacks and water bottles
with blankets and chairs
a listening ear
and a supply of bandages.

Bless the sidelines
where there's power
in witnessing others
share their gifts
learning how to work together,
surrounded by those who love them.

A Blessing for Parenting

You can find it in the reheated cups of coffee
the piles of laundry scattered around your house
underneath Lego creations and Barbie shoes
on the basketball court, the recital halls, and the pool lanes.

This blessing is for you,
your longing for peace,
the need for rest and renewal
the anger that clenches your teeth
the broken pieces of your heart.

This blessing whispers your name as you rock your baby
or comfort a scared child.

This blessing is there to reassure you
as you wade through paperwork
while you're on hold with doctors and offices,
as you sit next to your new driver.

This blessing is there when you need the words to calm and assure
this blessing marches into your home
and settles deep into the contours of your furniture
takes a seat at the breakfast table
wraps itself in a swaddle blanket.

This blessing swings and slides, skates and scooters
navigates the roads and school pick-up lines.
This blessing weaves into your words typed in the dark of night
scribbled in journals, receipts, and notepads
found amid endless Google docs and every list.

This blessing snaps along with every picture taken
and film developed
it's in every marker and paintbrush
and splash of color.

Turn your face to the sun
to its warmth
to renewal and hope
to the first green sprout
and let this blessing wash over you.

This blessing is yours,
made to make you feel safe, known
encouraged, and loved.

This blessing will fight for you,
it is within every breath you take
every step you take.

This blessing's words are written upon your heart:
You are a gift
You are strong
You are brave
You are worthy
You are loved.

Rest in this blessing
take deep breaths
and feel the love
that pulsates through your every move.

A Blessing for Cleaning

This blessing sees your reluctance
the hours you spend doing anything else
ignoring dust bunnies and dog hair
the overflowing dishes across the counter
and moving a pile of books and papers
to make room on the table to eat,
all to avoid the task of cleaning.

This blessing knows your time is stretched thin
that other jobs and work take your time
but also this blessing sees your frustration
while picking up another stray sock
and throwing away candy wrappers
stepping on Magna-Tiles and avoiding toppling blocks
trying to see through smudges and fingerprints
and toothpaste smeared on the bathroom mirror.

This blessing is here to help you
take one task at a time
one table cleared and washed
a load of laundry started
the kitchen counters sprayed.

This blessing wants you to know
that every task is holy
making a home for your family
creating safe and warm spaces
bringing comfort to rooms
making beds to be soft places to land.

May you see your work
and cleaning as a testament to love
caring for the people in your life,
praying for them
with each act of service.

In scrubbing floors,
may you remember the people who come into your home.

In washing dishes,
may you give thanks for full bellies.

In dusting shelves,
may you be surrounded by pictures and books.

In cleaning bathrooms,
may you celebrate the gift of bodies.

In washing clothes,
may you know the warmth of loving others.

What a gift to have a place to call home
and in every act of service and cleaning,
may God's presence shine.

A Blessing for the Library

Come on in,
this blessing says
you are welcome here,
there's no cost, no prerequisites
simply your presence
and a wish to immerse yourself in words and stories.

This blessing wants you to learn and ask questions
to seek answers from books and computers
to feel the turning of a page
and see covers and posters with your favorite characters.

This blessing knows the power of words
how they help us feel like we belong
and invite others to know they're welcome, too.

This blessing delights in small hands grabbing their first board books
new parents filling a library bag with classics from their childhood
librarians sharing their favorite book that sparks a reader's enthusiasm.

This blessing invites you to sit between the library stacks
to grab a pile of your favorites and get lost
to tell your parents and friends,
Come and see, you have to read this!

This blessing says, *Come on in*
for this library is yours
to get lost in a book
meet friends
take adventures to faraway lands
learn a new skill
draw, paint, and color
find a favorite author
sing and dance
watch stories come to life
and write your own.

But mostly, this blessing
sits beside you
encouraging you
inspiring you
reminding you of your power
found in reading and writing
to bring hope and joy to the world.

A Blessing for Reading with Your Children

As you read with your children
laughing with Piggie and Elephant
traveling to Narnia and Hogwarts,
may this blessing float through your words
as you feel their bodies press into yours
on your lap, a book shared between you
your daughter laying her hand on your knee
your son holding his Lego mini-figure, making and
remaking it,
may love stitch itself between you.

May the stories you read settle into your minds.
May they take you to vast and diverse lands to meet
everyday heroes.
May you meet and exchange ideas with people who have
transformed the world.

May you always remember
how it feels to be next to one another
listening and learning
bound to one another through words,
each other's safe space.

May the words uplift and encourage
may they make you think deeply and question widely
may they encourage you to keep learning.

May you always hold a book close for company
may you turn the pages and run your hands down the
book's spine
and trust that in every word and story you hear: *you are not
alone.*

A Blessing for Book Club

Come
gather around the table
with the aroma of chicken chili to greet you
bags and books, pen and paper scattered on the counter,
the waning sun's light pouring through the window.

Pull up a chair and choose a handful of your favorite snacks:
dark chocolate, pretzels, cheese and crackers
lather warm sourdough with butter,
release the week's worries

as you gather for the next hour
alongside your friends who have become like family,
women who love stories and staying up late for just one
more chapter,
people who know just the right book to recommend to cure
whatever ails you.

For those who long for more connection
for community rooted in the shared love of books,
may this blessing inspire you to go first
to form your own book club
to invite the woman you've seen reading while her children play
or the friend who always has a book in their bag
or the teacher who recommends the best books for your
kids.

May you linger with the lives before you
listening to their hopes and dreams,
may you write new stories together
may laughter be your shared language
may this chapter of book club be one to remember
and write about for years to come.

A Blessing for Those Who Travel

Bless all those who travel, Lord,
bless the early mornings and the late nights
the missed naps
the roadside stands
the twenty-four-hour gas stations
the audiobooks and screen time.

Open our eyes to the beauty of Your creation
teach us to marvel at the owl's nighttime music

and the hawk's wingspan soaring across the sky
the miles of farmland
or expansive skyscrapers.

In airports
along state highways
or high above the clouds
may our response be words of awe and praise,
How marvelous is your creation, Lord.

Bless us
when we find ourselves looking out
to the vastness of the ocean
or the top of a mountain
riding a streetcar on city streets
watching the setting sun,
and help us to hear your voice:
Be still, and know that I am God.

Open our eyes to the people we meet
seeing God in them
may we linger over shared experiences and stories,
our hearts in tune with the needs of others.

Help us to offer *Hello* and *How are you?*
with listening ears
help us to lend a hand to open a door
and slow our pace to not miss the smile of a child
or an artisan market with unique finds.

When our plans turn upside down
and we aren't sure which way to go
grant us patience and a humble heart.

When we are late or lost
tired or frustrated,
breathe Your Spirit into us.

The world has much to teach us
of kindness and compassion
reaching out to others
and helping friends in need.

Bless us and go with us, Lord,
wherever we go and in whatever we find,
teach us and inspire us.

Return us home safely
changed by your love,
and touched by the goodness of Your creation.

Goodnight Blessings

The nighttime routine with my children has varied with their ages and stages. A few constants have been reading and, of course, teeth brushing. There have been times when we've prayed before bed and ended with the Lord's Prayer. In other seasons, when later nights and early school mornings are upon us, we read one picture book and call it good.

But since their birth, one bedtime practice has remained constant: blessing them with the sign of the cross.

What a gift to hear the words of blessing every time we worship, and even more whenever we bless members of our family. And what a gift to remember that this is where we first and foremost find our calling: as children of God. Everything else stems from this love and grace. Everything flows from God having chosen us as God's people. Everything else filters through this lens of love and belonging. Throughout our lives we have multiple callings—son, daughter, friend, aunt, uncle, student, worker, parent. But each calling begins with God.

With my firstborn, I rock back and forth, my head against the chair, newborn Charlotte's small body leaning into mine, a glow coming from a small night-light across the room. Together we close our eyes to the sound of the noise machine and her on-again, off-again sucking. I watch her eyes flutter, and a drip of milk falls down her cheek.

When she's fallen into a deeper sleep, I place my finger on her forehead, making the sign of the cross. My finger moves down her forehead: "You are a loved child of God." Moving in the other direction I add, "And I love you."

We continue sitting for a few more minutes until I feel Charlotte's body go limp from sleep. I place her in the crib and back up slowly through her room.

The warmth of her forehead lingers on my fingertip.

We add one more child and soon our bedtime rituals with two young children are louder than when they were babies. Someone is always clamoring for a spot on my lap or fighting for who can hold the book. We gather on the couch, lean into one another, and read books. One of the kids will have a toy train, and then the other wants that same train. We turn to our prayers and ask one another who needs prayer. We name family and friends, teachers, and health workers. The dog. Mommy and Daddy. And then one kid takes the train out of the other's hand. Fighting ensues. I grab one child and put them in my lap, continuing to pray. My voice has to get louder to offset the arguments.

Finally, when I can't hold them any longer or my patience is frayed, I'll turn to each one and mark the sign of the cross on their forehead. "You are a loved Child of God," I tell them. Sometimes they turn their head and I'm left with their back. Other times they quickly reach their fingers toward me, marking a quick cross on my head.

No matter the struggle or the squirming, the blessing gets to them. Every night, they hear they are loved.

This is the gift of blessings—they go with us wherever we go. Throughout our lives they seep down into our bodies and spirits, they are part of how we live and breathe and move in the world.

Blessings don't need to be recited perfectly, but rather experienced as God's Spirit moving within us. I can't be at all places and times with my children, but the love I have for them and the love that God has for them *is* with them no matter what.

As you wrestle and wonder about your own calling and how you'll share your gifts and talents with others, may you rest in the truth that God sees us first as loved. May this love and these blessings guide you as you move through your days.

For the Places You've Been Called

From the beginning
the name is just a whisper
a question
Will you come?

May you step forward in trust
not knowing where you are going
or who you'll encounter
how you'll learn and change
and become more of who you are created
to be.

May you go
with wobbly knees
and unsteady steps
but forward all the same.

Put on courage and kindness
grab some extra water and a book for
company
don't forget pen and paper
to write your story
and the stories of those you meet.

As you go into the unknown
trust that the One who calls you
knows you and has already prepared a place for you.

A Blessing for Graduation

For anyone embarking on a new adventure,
this blessing is for you.

For anyone witnessing a loved one transitioning to something new,
this blessing is for you.

For those uncertain about the future
or where your path will take you,
this blessing is for you.

For anyone who has wondered where God is calling them,
this blessing is for you.

You are in a season of remembering what was:
late-night study sessions with friends
games and recitals
conversations with teachers.

A season to look back at where you've been
and the people and places who have shaped you.

In this season of letting go and holding on,
remember the love of God.

The God who formed you
who counts the hairs on your head
who dwells in you

who calls you a beloved child
and whose Spirit gives you strength and courage.

In this season of letting go and holding on
remember the radical love of Jesus:
Jesus who loves you as you are
who knows the pain and fear you experience
who walked with the lonely and forsaken
who took his love for the world to the cross
to bring us all to new life.

In this season of letting go and holding on
remember the presence of the Spirit
who infuses hope in your days
nourishes your parched soul
and gathers others to be your community and support.

In these days of joy and fear,
remember you are not alone.

Your path may seem clear
or perhaps uncertain,
yet either way you walk
and even in the steps that may feel foreign or backward,
you do not go alone.

Go forth in love.
Go forth and love.
Remember your name:
God's beloved.

A Blessing for a New Vocational Season

When your spirit feels uncertain
or a sense of unsettledness permeates your body

humming beneath the surface,
if you're waking up and wondering
is there more that I was made for?
God sees you.

When the workday trudges along
and the light you used to exude is dimmer,
you're restless and seeking greater challenge
with hours spent searching for new jobs,
God sees you.

When your conversations seem to be on a similar
loop
complaining about that protocol and this colleague
wondering how you can make more of a difference in the
world,
God sees you.

May you keep listening to the stirrings of your
heart
those moments where you feel alive
when someone compliments your gifts
where hours pass and you're fully present
when you find yourself smiling, take note,
God needs you and your gifts.

Every place you've been
the schooling you've completed
the work you participated in,
it's all been building toward where you are now,
nothing has been wasted
nothing will not be utilized
all those times you've adapted and pivoted
the lessons you've learned
have prepared you for this change to come.

In the wrestling and wondering—
Do I have what it takes?
Will I be too old or too young?
Can we afford this leap of faith?
What about all I've worked toward up until this point?
These questions are where God meets you,
to take one step at a time
one new class at a time
one job interview at a time
one conversation at a time
each step guided by the One who created you
to step forward in faith
walking into new experiences
and places where God has already gone before you.

A Blessing for Work

Bless the work of our hands
holding
caring
tending
writing
hammering
building
driving
farming
healing.

Bless the work of our mouths
speaking
teaching
preaching
encouraging
reading
singing.

Bless the work of our hearts
consoling
forgiving
worshipping
loving.

Give us courage
to walk paths where others have not
to blaze trails of inclusion
to seek out the lost and lonely
to listen with our whole bodies
to seek compromise
and to continually bring peace.

Give us strength for the road ahead
trusting that where we are called,
we go with God's presence.

In every word we offer,
may we speak with compassion.

In every work we do,
may we recognize the humanity of others.

In every task we complete,
may we see God's presence.

May we be people
who serve others
and offer ourselves
who step in when others fall away
who work for the common good
and treasure the people before us.

A Blessing for Caregivers

Maybe you're bone-tired and compassion-fatigued
from caring for others
for all the times you've been the driver
to doctors' visits and pharmacies
grocery runs and therapy
from washing dishes and laundry
wiping foreheads and disinfecting sheets
preparing breakfast, lunch, and dinner
and organizing pills,
God sees your work.

Maybe you're dreaming of a break
of real rest from constant worry and stress
a break from being the one to handle
all the schedules and who needs to be where,
rest from managing others' emotions
while being the one to pass on information and updates
and keeping your feelings bottled up,
God sees your work.

Maybe you're unsure how this came to be
that your life revolves around another
your schedule dictated by the needs of someone else
bearing the brunt of their anger and pain
knowing all the side effects of medicine
that wreak havoc on a body you love,
God sees your work.

Your care and love
do not go unnoticed,
may your offerings of healing be multiplied.

May the tenderness you offer,
also land on you.

May you feel God's compassion
wrap around your body
like a well-loved quilt.

Close your eyes
and hear God's words to you:
Well done, good and faithful servant.

A Blessing for the Days of Raising Children

These are the days I live for
windows open, leaves dancing in the wind
the light reflecting on the dogwood blooms and
 redbuds
squirrels scurrying up trees to a chorus of grasshoppers.

Filling water bottles and packing bags
chopping fruits and peeling potatoes
doling out snacks and helping with math homework
friends ringing the doorbell to play
walks through town greeting anyone you pass.
Surrounded by books on the couch
Scrabble at the dining room table
dinner together
catch in the front yard.

Stringing words one after another
weaving stories and sharing hope
finding solace in a novel.

These are the days I live for
over and over
the ones right in front of me
mine for the taking
living for the days with the ones I love.

A Blessing for Women

This one is for the women
the mothers and daughters
aunts and nieces
friends and community members
the ones we look up to
and link arms with
walking side by side.

Bless the women
who are with us when we walk uncertain
when we don't know which way to turn
when we need a hand or a shoulder
when we need a kind word
when we need a convicting word
when we need a homemade meal
when we need someone to sing with us
when we need a hand-stitched quilt.

Bless the women
who offer their expertise and time
paving a way forward
where all women are acknowledged for their skills
and no position is too far out of reach.

Bless the women
who rock our babies

and share their snacks
who pick up our kids when we're running late
and make them feel at home.

Bless the women
who text us to check in
and pray unceasingly for us
who remember that painful anniversary
and sit with us when there are no words.

Bless the women
who know when we're lying
and we actually do need help
the ones who walk in and know where the cleaning supplies are
and put away the dishes
and offer their presence.

Bless the women
who sign up and show up
who run PTOs and board meetings
who stay up late finishing their education classes.

Bless the women
who feed and prepare snacks
who make meal plans and do the grocery shopping
who remember to fill out the permission form
and practice math problems at the table.

Bless the women
who make the desserts
and stay late to clean up
who hold all the schedules in their head
and make sure everyone is where they need to be.

Bless the women
who sit and cry with us
the ones who sing and pray with us
the ones who know that we're better together.

May we continually bless these women,
and may we be these women.

A Blessing for Poetry

A turn of a phrase
a pause
one single word
attention to detail—
poetry has much to teach us.

Train our eyes to see the way words dance
and open our ears to the cadence of each stanza
inspire us with earth's beauty and mystery
comfort us with rhythms and rhymes
help us to attune our ways
to see beneath the surface.

May we bring hope to others
inviting moments to slow down
and see the poetry of our lives.

A Blessing for Teachers

Blessed are the teachers
the ones who come in early and stay late
who work weekends
planning and grading
praying for their students

worrying and wondering
whether they're doing enough.

Blessed are the teachers
who see the student with their head low
and offer a warm smile
and speak the words: *I'm so glad to see you*
the ones who study and read and take extra classes
learning the best techniques
and how to meet each student where they are
who know which kids need a friend
and the buddy packs of food for the weekend
and the students whose only relief is found in the school building.

Blessed are the teachers
who take on other duties:
dressing in character
morning dance party coordinator
nose-wiper and bandage-wrapper.

Blessed are the teachers
who field emails from parents
prep for state tests
decorate bulletin boards
answer questions:
Can I go to the bathroom?
When is this due?
Is this for a grade?

Blessed are the teachers
loving and raising up leaders
our hope and heart for the future.

A Blessing for Remembering Parenthood

Grab your cozy fleece blanket and find a seat among the
crumbs
step over Hot Wheels tracks, boots, scarves, and coats
push the stuffies and books aside to make room on the couch,
come and sit and remember.

Remember the first milestones—
the lost tooth and that gap-toothed grin of your youngest
the smiling pictures on the first day of school
the teenagers with their arms crossed, brooding
waiting for the picture to be over.

Remember the first words—*mama, dada, bubba*
first foods—messy faces covered in mashed banana and
avocado
the driving lessons with clenched fists
the joy of a first goal, basket, and touchdown.

Remember the sleepless nights—
hours rocking your baby and pacing the halls
the prayers echoed in the dark under a moonlit sky
nursing till both of your eyes closed
researching symptoms and programs and schools.

Remember the hours in the car—
overhearing secrets and gossip of who likes who
audiobooks and podcasts
and singing at the top of your lungs with the windows
down.

Remember the moments of connection—
making wooden block creations and blanket forts

dressing up for tea parties
after-dinner dancing and hours reading books.

Remember gathering at the table—
spaghetti-covered faces and syrup-sticky hands
sharing highs and lows from the day
lighting candles
setting a place for the friend from down the street
passing the plate of brownies
leaving leftovers for the kids at practice and the parents who work late.

Remember the friends and playgroups—
trying to have a conversation between cries and requests for drinks and snacks
the friends who text: *I'll be right there*
and who know your sweet indulgence without asking
the text threads that last for days about rashes
and *Why won't my kid eat anything other than mac and cheese?*
You too? and
I'm glad we're not the only ones.

What do you see?
What do you hear?
What do you feel?

Remember the years
you lived and loved
laughed and cried
hoped and prayed.

Your community and this world
are better because of your love.

A Blessing for the Ones Who Show Up

This is for the ones
who are the first to arrive
who turn on the percolator
open doors and windows
let the light in
who scrub counters and pick up toys
who set the tables
and welcome everyone by name
the ones who sit with the newcomer
making sure no one is alone.

Bless the ones who show up
in texts and phone calls
with a warm embrace
and a shoulder to cry on
with your favorite drink
and time to ask *how are you*?
and stay to listen for the answer.

Bless the ones
who just walk in
make themselves at home
who fold laundry with you
and share their kids' snacks
the ones who remember
birthdays and anniversaries
and the power in showing up.

Thank you for these friends,
bless these friends.

Make it so we are these friends.

A Blessing for Small Towns

Blessed are the small towns
where healing and hope
dance in the streets
to local musicians
and children play freeze tag
and greet their friends
where restaurants and stores donate food and time
where neighbors share a meal
and open their hearts in generosity.

Blessed are the small towns
where the words
cancer
grief
loss
sickness
medical bills
are no match
for the power of community.

Blessed are the ones who proclaim:
We're in this together
You're not alone
This is our home
These are our people
This is community.

A Blessing for Neighbors

That we may step out our doors
and into our streets
saying hello

walking through parks
asking the name of the immigrant family who recently
moved in
knowing the professions of the people next door
the ages and interests of their kids
inviting the widower for dinner
and sharing store-bought donuts on the porch
with the couple down the street.

That we tend to shared spaces
throwing away garbage
sharing extra produce
offering to watch the kids
picking up groceries for the homebound
raking and bagging fallen leaves
collecting the mail for a traveling friend
and shoveling a snowy driveway.

That we venture to different communities
learning new traditions and cultures
asking questions and really listening to learn
seeing where people are lacking in food, shelter, and safety
and how to come together
for mutual thriving.

That we watch friendships grow and change over years
children running freely between houses
front doors opening and closing
with a welcome and knowing each kid by name
grabbing chairs and sitting on the lawn
or around a firepit
sharing stories and challenges
no competition just compassion
and the gift of being known.

A Blessing for Leadership

Where are our leaders
where are those that lead with love and
kindness
who believe in the common good
who seek dialogue and understanding
who cross aisles of division
and bring people together?

Where are our leaders
who understand we need one another
and that the least of these
are the ones from whom we can learn
that differences can be met with compassion?

May we raise leaders
steeped in kindness
aware of the strength in listening to others,
who take time to make eye contact
and know that behind every person
is a story worth learning.

May we take our leadership
out of the realm of comments, likes, and social media
posts
where every word tries to one-up the other
and people never talk face-to-face
but with only the tap of their fingers on a screen.

Guide us in our homes to cultivate
opportunities to disagree
to debate and listen
to learn of another's perspective.

Guide us in our communities
to seek out the stranger
to learn of their lives
and the ways they've been shaped.

Guide us in our world
to see how vastly interconnected we are
that when someone goes hungry
we all suffer,
that when someone loses their livelihood
we all hurt.

Give us courage
to keep standing up for good
in the face of injustice
when people are turned away
due to the color of their skin.

Give us strength
to keep fighting the good fight
even when we lose hope
and the arc of justice feels so far away.

Encourage us to keep leaning in
and fighting for a world
where leaders are known first and
    foremost
by their kindness.

A Blessing for Protesting

Love
Not hate
Makes America great

The voices join together
neither the rain
nor the cold
will keep the people from assembling
from protecting
from coming together
from standing up and speaking out
from believing that justice will prevail.

Bless the ones who walk and chant
and raise their signs
empower them to keep showing up
and remembering those
whose voices have been silenced.

Standing on capitol steps
help us remember those who have paved the way
who have fought and defended our country
who have not yet grown weary of causing good trouble
and believe that we can make our country
the home of the free
and a land for all.

This is what democracy looks like.

A Blessing for Election Day

Fill our hearts and intentions
our motives and thoughts with compassion
hope for the despairing
healing for the sick
justice for the oppressed
calm for the anxious
peace for the restless.

Open our hearts to listen
for your song of hope
discerning how to provide affordable healthcare
finding funding for childcare and mental health
creating safe neighborhoods
and in all that affects our communities,
keep our attention fixed on you, Lord.

Wherever we go this day,
may we go with peace.

Whoever we encounter,
may we greet them in peace.

In all that we do and say,
may all our actions point to the One
who brings hope and healing for the world.

Keep us fixed on Jesus,
who embodied love and a servant heart.

When we go to sleep this night,
may we remember
that in our waking and sleeping
in rising again to a new day,
You are God—
the God who calls us Your beloved children
a God of justice and peace
a God of healing and wholeness
a God who brings hope
and delivers mercy,
a God ushering in a kingdom
where love reigns
forever and always.

A Blessing for a Changing Body

Bless the bodies that are changing
in small and large ways—
new pain in the knee
shortness of breath as we climb hills
the surprise at seeing ourselves in the mirror
with more wrinkles and thinning hair.

Bless these bodies.
May we be empowered
to claim the ages and stages of our body
the gray hairs
the extra weight
the stiffness
the tired eyes.

May all our changes be celebrated
a recognition of days well-lived and experienced
a body capable of tending to life
a body that has grown and stretched and strengthened.

This blessing hears our sighs
and it's with us when the nights are long
with new aches and pains.

This blessing breathes into us
reminders of our strength and beauty
and our body's ability to adapt and change.

May we be gentle and curious
not hiding who we are
or how our body is changing
but seeing every part of ourselves
as holy and good.

A Blessing for a Funeral Visitation

If you're feeling alone
if you're grieving
if you're wondering how to make it through the days
if your home reminds you of all you have lost,
this blessing is for you.

Remember the hands reaching for a hug
the embraces and tears
the memories shared and laughter remembered.

Remember how on a single night
a thousand stories came together
to bear testament to love and life.

May you trust this abundance
and lean on the community
to help you remember
and be with you as you grieve
and to walk with you toward a new normal.

When you want to feel close to your loved one
look no further than this visitation
the line of people who gathered
who were made better by knowing them
whose lives are richer thanks to this connection.

May you continue to sing and pray
and when your voice is just a whisper
or unable to be heard,
remember the prayers and people who hold you in
    your grief.

A Blessing for Bearing Witness to a Friend

Sometimes the connection happens over the phone
or with a text or handwritten letter
maybe on a walk
or on the sidelines of a baseball game.
Perhaps while waiting in the school pick-up line
you have an opportunity to really hear a friend.

May you be the friend who notices
the red-rimmed eyes
hunched shoulders
a look of weariness
and who reaches out with a kind word.

May you be the friend
who picks up the phone
who drops other plans
and asks, *How are you really doing?*

May you listen with your whole body
more eager to hear than to speak
to let silence be a means of comfort
with a hand ready to hold.

Don't offer judgment or advice,
but the reminder that your friend is not alone.

May you acknowledge the sadness present
and the strength they show
the courage within them
the gift that they are.

In bearing witness to your friend,
may you listen and not shy away.

May you look your friend in the eyes
allowing your presence to speak
that whatever is to come
and whatever has and will befall them,
you will be by their side.

A Blessing for Not Losing Hope

It takes one spark—
maybe a phone call
or text message
words of solidarity:
Me too
This isn't right
I feel alone
I'm scared
What's going on?
What can we do?

Then you meet one-on-one
walking and sharing
working out the stress
moving your body and your mind
nodding along in agreement
with every step, realizing
others are with you.

You've lamented and questioned
you've cried and raged
now channel it all toward a common ground
rooted in listening and unity.

May this conversation be the start of many
where voices are shared and heard
stories lifted up and friendships forged.

May we stick to the truth
that we need one another
and when we have lost our voice,
may the voices of courage carry us through
chanting and singing and standing for a future
where justice and truth reign
and will not be overcome.

Give us a spirit of gentleness
to be open
to have a posture of humility
and to see those gathered at the table
as belonging to us.

You're Always Welcome to Pray Here

An hour north of Minneapolis, where the skyscrapers have been replaced by wildflowers and glistening lakes, and the prairie grass sways in the wind, lives a community of prayer. At St. John's Abbey, a community devoted to monastic life, the monks live, work, pray, and serve together. They welcome visitors into their sacred spaces to experience a life rooted in prayer.

I've spent many days retreating at St. John's Abbey. A core experience of every visit includes joining the monks for their daily prayer. Sitting in the stillness of the sanctuary, the bell tolling, I watch the brothers enter one by one in their black robes. At their seats, they bow their heads to the cross.

I let the soft chanting wash over me. I also look into the eyes of the monks: eyes that look tired, even possibly bored, bodies that most likely came from hours of work, minds that probably ponder the tensions and events of the day. In a sense, they hold the feelings and emotions of everyone else who gathers to pray with them. But they are here. They show up and will show up day after day, hour after hour, to pray. And if they can't find the strength to muster the words at that moment, the community around them will pray on their behalf.

In my visits to the abbey, I don't make it to every prayer time, but the monks never fail to show up. Isn't that a gift? Somewhere, someone is praying for you and for the world. Someone is holding space for the aches you hold and the yearnings of your heart. Someone is pleading on your behalf for healing and wholeness.

The monks inspire me to keep coming to God with my fumbling prayers and my early morning yawns when I'm wrestling with belief.

This is what the church calendar does for us, too, as Christians—it points us to the larger story and work of God. The liturgical year also connects us to others who are following the same calendar. We have a God that is in, above, and beyond all time. Yet we need markers to guide us through this world and our faith. The church year helps us do that, and brings us into community with others.

I wish I could sit across the table with you and ask what prayers you're holding. What makes your heart sing and what keeps you up at night. What I can do is hold space for you. And I can point you to the truth that our prayers never go unheard. I can remind you that someone is praying for you. And I can encourage you to come with your prayers, doubts, fears, and joys, and lay them before God. I can offer words of blessings that meet you in your wrestling and wondering. I can assure you that God hears you.

The following blessings invite you to dwell in the seasons of the church year. Move with the rhythm of God's time. Center yourself in the stories of God's love and redemption. Remember that as you honor the seasons, you are also joining a host of others marking this time.

A Blessing for the Ones Who Tell the Stories

Blessed are the ones who tell the story,
God's story of hope and healing
God's story of a people in need of a savior
God's story of creation and redemption.

Blessed are the ones who share the story over and over,
in funny accents and with hand movements
with song and dance
who pour over pages in study and prayer
who learn history, Greek, and Hebrew
and understand how to break down big ideas.

Blessed are the ones who share the story
from pulpits and dining room tables
across Sunday school classrooms and park benches
in the early morning hours and late at night
over text messages and written notes.

Blessed are the ones who tell the story,
who need to hear it for themselves
who soak in God's word with every retelling
with every question and answer,
the ones who never tire of sharing the Good News.

Blessed are the ones who doubt and wrestle
who search for God's love even as they extend it to others
who struggle themselves over which way to turn
or how to forgive.

Blessed are the hearers of the Word,
may they have open ears
and a willing spirit.

May they let the words become them
infused in their soul
an outpouring of
love
grace
forgiveness
hope.

Blessed is the One,
who first breathed the story into existence.

A Blessing for Advent

This season is waiting for you,
to welcome you into the warmth
to settle your soul
to light a fire within you.

You, too, are waiting,
for healing and wholeness
for compassion
for understanding differences.

Take your time this Advent,
to savor the sounds of the season
the crackle of a fire
dough being mixed and kneaded
well-worn Bible pages turning.

Take your time to see the gifts of the season,
lights twinkling
the evergreen from an Advent wreath
red-and-white striped wrapping paper
kids dressed as angels and shepherds for a Christmas
program.

Take your time to touch this season,
the warmth of your children's hands
a warm bowl of chili
bread and wine offered at communion
water on your fingertips from the baptismal
font.

Take your time to taste this season,
fruitcake and eggnog
milk chocolate opened each day from an Advent
calendar
sugar cookies decorated with sprinkles and icing.

Take your time to feel this season,
hope tinged with doubt
the resonance of music
the wooden figures of a nativity.

The season is waiting for you,
brimming with God's goodness
come and wait
and see.

A Blessing for Christmas

This blessing is for the weary rejoicers,
the ones singing *Joy to the World*
and proclaiming the *Lord is come*
but wondering if Christmas has come for them.

This blessing is for the weary rejoicers,
clinging to hope
that the birth of a baby
in a dirty manger
can truly be their joy.

This blessing is for the weary rejoicers,
lighting candles in the darkness
singing songs of love coming down
praying for peace on earth.

For those decorating trees and homes
baking treats and drinking hot chocolate
and grasping ahold of any hope
that Jesus came for them.

This blessing is for the weary rejoicers,
peering into the manger
missing their loved ones
fearing their own health
concerned about violence both near and far
but gazing upon the baby born
a new hope dawning.

Whether we believe or doubt,
Christ is born for us.

Whether we're joyful or sorrowful,
Christ is born for us.

Christmas comes to us all,
both the weary and ready.

May we never grow tired of this mystery.
May we never grow too old to believe.
May we never forget the beauty of a baby.
May we never fail to bring gifts to the Savior.
May we never fail to stand in awe of God's presence.

May we never forget the joy,
even as we cry out in weariness.

A Blessing for Epiphany

Epiphany arrives in the dark of night
under a moonlit sky
following the hopes of travelers
searching for a star
longing for a Prince of Peace
waiting to meet the savior.

Epiphany reveals a baby
cradled in love
wrapped in Mary's arms
gazed upon by Joseph
nuzzled by animals
born on a night long ago
and also born anew in hearts every day.

Epiphany follows the love of this baby into the world
into deep pain and heartache
to be a light for all
sharing gifts of forgiveness
and light that reaches to the farthest corners of the earth.

Epiphany speaks to us
not with loud shouts
but whispers *come and see*
have a seat
rest a while
listen to stories of love manifest
here and now.

Epiphany walks long roads
seeking to lift up the lonely
to share food with the hungry

to heal a broken heart
to witness Jesus's miracles.

Epiphany shines now
as brightly as on the night of Jesus's birth
shining for our homes, neighborhoods, and
world,
may we continue to reflect this light
and be the face of Jesus to those we meet.

A Blessing for Saying Goodbye to the Alleluias

This one is for the fatigued
the ones who can't utter another prayer
or bring themselves to feel joy.

For the ones reading the news and wondering:
How did we get here?
How will we get out of here?
Who have we become?
Are we safe?
Is anyone safe?

This one is for those
wading through treatments and insurance claims
caregivers running into endless needs
parents tracking symptoms and delayed milestones
friends watching a loved one battle addiction
families facing loss of income.

We offer our final alleluias
we bury them or box them up
we sing, pray, and shout alleluia one last time—for now.

And we turn to the One
who doesn't need our alleluias or any words
just simply us, as we are.

The One who meets us in the darkness
and our absence of joy
the One who carries our broken alleluias into the wilderness.

A Blessing for Ash Wednesday

Today we remember
our lives
and our deaths
we face mortality
and that of our loved ones.

Today we remember
how we have been formed in dust
and will return to the earth.

Today the mark of the cross
written in ashes
graces our foreheads
for all to see
reminding us of our fragility
sickness and pain
grief and loss
heartache and brokenness,
all of life
but a whisper of what is to come.

Today may we sit in the truth
that we will die
and may we not run from the sadness

and what could have been
or what-ifs
but hear the words wash over us,
ashes to ashes
dust to dust.

May we see the cross smeared on foreheads
and recognize our common humanity
and our common mortality
so that we approach others and this world
with gentleness
reverence for our place among God's people
here now
created in love.

May we trust that out of the dust,
beauty rises.

May we believe that out of the dust,
hope emerges.

A Blessing for Lent

God of mystery and wisdom,
be with us this Lenten season.

The way has been long already
sickness, worry, isolation, fear, waiting
our hearts are heavy
our souls are exhausted
our bodies are hurting
our hope is wavering
yet, You are with us.

God of mystery and wisdom,
be with us this Lenten season.

Show us Your grace
in the small moments of silence
the prayers offered
the kindness of a stranger
the lighting of a candle
the listening to a friend,
You are with us.

God of mystery and wisdom,
be with us this Lenten season.

Settle our hearts
revive our spirits
increase our faith
spread our love.

God of mystery and wisdom,
be with us this Lenten season.

In ashes and dust
reading and listening
wandering and walking
praying and singing
eating and fasting,
show us the way forward.

God of mystery and wisdom,
be with us this Lenten season.

As we walk to the cross
keep our eyes fixed

on You and Your love
caring for others
crossing boundaries
reaching out to the poor
taking our pain
transforming death into life
over and over again.

God of mystery and wisdom,
be with us this Lenten season.

A Blessing for Palm Sunday

It's time to wave the palms
and walk to Jerusalem,
we know the story and where we're heading
but we're already facing so many deaths
so much loss and uncertainty,
do we need more?

Let us toss down our coats
our apathy
our self-righteousness
and our own plans
to seek the common good.

We're marching to Jerusalem,
but also to the neighbors across the street
the jail across the ocean
to war-torn Palestine and Ukraine
to the halls of our capitol.

Give us humbleness
may we turn over peace

again and again
until all people can shout,
blessed is He who comes
blessed are we
the free.

A Blessing for Holy Week

If you feel as though life is already dark
if Lent feels never-ending
if worry has taken over your mind
if you wonder when dawn will break,
this blessing is for you.

This blessing gently invites you
to feel the week
the holy days
the lingering minutes
the stories of our faith.

This blessing knows uncertainty, pain, and darkness,
but this blessing also sees the light.

This blessing will take your hand and guide you
to receive the bread and wine
hearing the words *given and shed for you*,
to cradle your feet and wash them
looking in your eyes with love and a servant's heart,
to sit at the foot of the cross crying with you
offering presence in grief and loss
never leaving your side.

To wait and dance in the dark,
peering into the light

rising with the Son,
meeting at the empty tomb.

This blessing is yours
through the holiest of days
and the biggest heartbreaks,
this blessing is yours
transforming death into life.

Come closer and hear these words
they are yours
today and everyday:
You are loved, you are loved, you are loved.

A Blessing for the Empty Tomb

Come and peer into the empty tomb
step inside
feel the moisture drip on your forehead
squint your eyes and adjust to the dawning
    light
feel the darkness
listen to the silence
don't ask too many questions
just look and see the emptiness
grab on to the hope of something more
hope that can't be found in the tomb
or locked up
or coerced with fear and violence.

No, this hope is floating and soaring
spanning the heights
calling and dancing for the world
life and love and joy

it's everything that comes after death
so save your questions
and bask in the Son
who knows you
who cannot be contained
even by death.

May this emptiness propel us forward
to know the end is just the beginning.

A Blessing for Easter

Easter
announces itself
under the cover of darkness
a starlit night
animals rustling in the forests
owls keeping watch in the trees.

Easter
arises with the sun
the small, slow footsteps of women
carrying tears and burdens
cradling lost hope
wondering what could have been.

Easter
opens to an empty tomb
a discarded blanket
mixed with blood and tears
tossed aside.

Easter
runs with Good News

declares to all who will listen
shouts to the heavens
proclaims the goodness of creation.

Easter
is like the sparkling of water in shades of blue and
  aquamarine
the dance of green grass
the opening of crocus flowers
the sound of a frog's chorus.

Easter
reaches from the emptiness
to find our longing
desires
hopes
and pulls us through
the depths of loss
grief
and death.

Easter
shows us
our lives
found
in God.

A Blessing for Pentecost

The world seems on fire
yet not in ways that build and encourage,
but in tearing down others for their
  beliefs
and building walls that separate.

Show us the way of Pentecost's fire
with rushing wind and eclectic voices
coalescing to build common ground
and expanding tables.

Help us to know the fire of your Spirit
enliven our lives with a burning desire,
to share peace, justice, and love
listening to different languages
celebrating cultures in all their beauty and color,
learning about the God who speaks across borders and divides.

Help us to know the breath of your Spirit
and spark moments of connection
between people of varying faiths and walks of life,
so that neighbors can walk side by side
not seeking to change minds
but to change our minds about how we can be together in
community.

Help us to know the beauty of your Spirit
drawing together with multitudes of people and languages
coming together to feast
coming together to understand one another
and to be understood.

Help us to know the beauty of one another
where we don't shy away from differences
but speak up when another's humanity is demeaned.

Pentecost blows in
with the Spirit ready and willing
to lift up believers
to rush in with peace.

May we be people
who see and honor
God's Spirit in others
who reach out in unity
and celebrate differences.

May we trust the Spirit
even when we can't trust ourselves
and are learning to trust others.

A Blessing for Ordinary Time

There's nothing ordinary about a mother's love
the way she knows what each babble and grunt of her baby means
how she holds her child against her chest, feeding while everyone else sleeps
how she cuts her kids' sandwiches in just the right way
and packs the extra snacks and drinks for after practice
or stays up late into the night searching for what *that* symptom means
and the way she holds a cool cloth on a forehead
and prays endlessly for their safety and peace
when she blesses them as they head off to school
and embraces them as soon as they walk into their homes
sits patiently at the dining room table as they recite multiplication facts
and says *I know it's hard* when a friend is unkind
or a thousand other ways that a mother shows up every minute of every day.

There's nothing ordinary about the changing seasons
the way nature prepares for what's to come
one day ice-covered trees and the next a tiny shoot

crocus plants bursting from the newly thawed garden
roots talking to one another underground
resting and growing and being anything but idle
how the bears, snakes, and frogs know when to burrow deep
  away from the cold
and the monarch butterfly arrives back with a flutter of
  their wings
or a thousand other ways that nature continues to flourish
  every minute of every day.

There's nothing ordinary about life in the church
the way the words of a hymn
"Amazing Grace" and "Be Thou My Vision" speak right to
  your heart
how the Lord's Prayer comes to your memory after years of
  not reciting it
how old and young sit next to one another, shake hands and
  say *Peace Be With You*
that when one person can't pray due to overwhelming
  sadness and grief
the woman next door prays for them
that candles being lit and pleas for peace form common
  ground
and children read Bible lessons for all to hear
the woman learning to play the guitar for the first time
  shares her gifts as an offering
coins make a noise as they are collected for local food
  pantries
how belief and doubt mix and sit next to each other
and a thousand other ways that God's love
is made manifest in the ordinary people
showing up week after week.

May we never forget the small
seemingly ordinary

moments of our days
and how extraordinary
it is to be among
God's creation and God's people.

A Blessing for the Table

Come to the table
where all are welcome
friends and family
young and old
believers and doubters.

May you find a table
waiting for you
with a place set
labeled with your name
a soft seat to rest
water at the ready
and comfort food to feed your body and soul.

At the table,
may you remember those who are hungry
in body and spirit,
those thirsting for a friend
to listen and hear their burdens.

May your home
have a table with plenty of seats
so doors and hearts can be opened,
and teach us to embrace all
who come with open arms.

May we be fed not only with food
but laughter and joy

shared between generations
of families and friends
and may we feast
on kindness and compassion
seeing with eyes of peace.

May we be relentless in our welcome.

A Blessing for Communion

May you see
your own hunger
the needs you can't share with anyone
the hurts you've kept buried
and release them to God as you come to the table,
trusting that you will be met with mercy
and seen as only God can see you,
fully loved just as you are.

Come and feast
on grace and forgiveness
to gather with all God's people
in need of mercy
standing side by side
with open hands
and shattered hearts.

May you taste
the sweetness of communion
with no need to perform or work
to earn God's favor.

May you remember that communion doesn't just happen
at the table
but also with the gathering of friends for a meal

or a picnic in the park
toddlers sharing their snacks
fast food and iced tea dropped off to a drained parent
birthday treats at a party
cookies and milk after the school day.

It's bread and wine
friendship and laughter
sharing and confessing
forgiving and being forgiven
listening and talking
praying and silence.

It's the world in need of togetherness
for places where all are welcomed and accepted
where differences are celebrated
reconciliation worked toward
hard conversations spoken with grace.

Come and eat
take and receive
be fed
know love
and be sent
fulfilled and nourished
so that you, then,
can fill others.

May you experience God's wide welcome.

A Blessing for Vacation Bible School

This blessing is for the volunteers,
the ones who pour hours into planning, preparing,
    decorating, and leading

the ones who pray for the kiddos who will attend
and for the children who need a safe space to spend their
evenings
the volunteers who dress up to sing and dance
the ones who act out Bible stories
and burn their fingers on hot glue (again)
the ones who hand out water and cookies
the ones who can't get *that* song out of their head.

This blessing is for the parents,
who entrust their children to the church
so they can be immersed in God's love and grace
who pray for volunteers, pastors, and worship leaders
who turn up the catchy songs in their car
and have dance parties in the living room
and find glitter and crafts scattered around the house.

This blessing is for the children,
the ones who jump, dance, and sing
and the ones sitting quietly waiting for a friend
the ones who can recite the Bible stories by heart
and the ones hearing it for the first time
for the elementary kids full of joy
and the middle schoolers who roll their eyes and feel too
cool.

This blessing rejoices in the stories that inspire
and teach kindness and love
for the crafts that hang on walls
the snacks that nourish hungry bellies
and the games that tire energetic bodies.

This blessing hopes that the songs sung
seep deep into hearts and minds

so that the words and truth
become as close as breath.

This blessing is for all who remember their youth,
summers at church learning God's story and feeling God's love
and for the ones searching for a place to be welcomed.

This blessing shouts for joy
for the God who delights in us
calls us beloved
and brings us into community.

A Blessing for All Saints

As the leaves fall
and the air turns crisp,
as the ground prepares for rest
and the light fades,
November reminds us
to trust the rhythm of nature.

On All Saints,
we recognize the saints among us
feasting at our tables
dancing in our aisles
singing to the heavens.

On All Saints,
we remember those who have died
whose spirits and souls comfort us.
Give us space to pause and reflect,
grant us moments to feel your presence
to open ourselves to the connections
between this world and the next.

May we remember to be saints,
help us seek your light in all that we do
and in all that we say,
offering your grace and hope
to those who stumble
to the chronically ill in need of a listening ear
to the friend seeking forgiveness
and a world in need of peace,
give us a moment to breathe and reflect
to open ourselves to the wideness of your mercy.

A Blessing for a Well-Worn Faith

May your faith be worn
like an old red hymnal
faded with wrinkled edges
a coffee-stained cover and tear-soaked pages,
all reminders of being well-loved.

May your faith, like a red hymnal
hold close the hymns of your youth
singing them by heart
to be recalled when grief and doubt creep in
and all other words fail you.

May your hands cradle this treasure
and feel deep within
all the other hands that have held this book.

May you know that your faith comes from a long
history
and has transformed and comforted
perplexed and challenged
men and women for centuries.

Nothing hasn't been asked before
and nothing is too hard or too big
or too small for God to carry.

So reach out your hands
grasp the hymnal
feel the faith of others
pulsing through its pages
singing for you
offering a song of hope.

A Blessing for Loving Others

Help us to love *that* neighbor
with the annoying dog who barks at all hours
the children who bully and name-call
the family who leaves their garbage scattered on the street
the stranger who sleeps on the park bench
the homes displaying opposing political signs.

Help us to love
those we disagree with
the ones who would never step foot
in our churches or homes,
those we probably wouldn't invite inside either.

When the world finds itself
more willing to connect through screens
when fingers type responses at the speed of our anger and frustration
devoid of thoughtfulness and care
when polarization is the norm
and common ground hard to find

may we learn to slow down
look up and see the people right in front of us.

That in others, we may see with the eyes of God
each person crossing our paths
no matter belief or color or party
all created in God's image
full of goodness
rich in experiences and stories.

Equip us to engage in dialogue
to not focus on changing opinions
but creating space for storytelling and connection.

May we take small steps toward
those we consider different
may we offer a wave and hello
bake sweet treats to share
ask *how are you?* and really listen
learn first names and then use them.

May we find ourselves in groups with diverse opinions
book clubs, PTO meetings, Bible studies, and playdates
meeting one another with a smile and openness
knowing we can learn so much from others.

May our hope be found in one another
all image-bearers of God,
this is the hope for our world
this is the hope for our children.

A Blessing for Remembering Your Baptism

When the world feels upside down
and you don't know where you fit in
or how you belong
and you can't seem to believe in yourself,
take hold of this blessing.

For this blessing knows you
from before you were born
numbering your hairs
knitting you together
dwelling in your bone and marrow
loving you from the beginning.

This blessing heard your first cries
and leaned in close
as your mother held you on her chest
and you opened your eyes to see
love looking down at you.

This blessing is in every drip of water
and in the sign of the cross
in the friends and family who stand up
and open their arms in welcome
with voices singing "Amazing Grace" and "Jesus Loves You."

This blessing sees you through
questions of belief
and the doubts that cloud your vision
in every wondering it draws you closer,
this blessing knows the pain of broken alleluias
and amens whispered under breath

the prayers screamed to the void
and in picking up the pieces of a broken heart.

This blessing washes over you
as you get ready for the day
in sipping a cool glass of water
stomping your feet in a puddle
jumping in the pool
tipping your head to the falling rain,
with every sip and splash
the reminder of God's love
pouring over you.

This blessing knows that your name
of God's beloved
wasn't just for one time
but for all time
from before the cosmos were formed
till beyond anything we can fathom.

So don't forget or lose hope
you've been called and claimed
drenched in the waters of God's grace.

GETTING LOST

What Country Are We In?

I wake atop a borrowed blanket, feeling the hard earth and loose sticks against my back. My fellow Peace Corps travelers and I have gone two days without a shower as we have hiked over the mountains of Guinea, West Africa, into Senegal. My fingernails have streaks of dirt underneath. Our next mode of transport will be a bus, but we overestimate our capabilities through the African mountains. We stop well past dark in a small remote village where the village chief takes us in for the night. This is where we sleep, next to one another, and unsure of our location. "What country are we in?" I ask, as a cool breeze rustles the leaves.

"We'll never have to ask that question again in our lives," my friend says and we both laugh. Here we are in either Senegal or Guinea after a week of hiking on vacation. Soon, though, we'll be making our way back home to our work as Peace Corps Volunteers in The Gambia. Our hosts take us to the buses and send us on our way in peace, but it will be another two days before I rest my head back in my hut in The Gambia, my home for the last year.

Transport in West Africa works on a different speed—the bus (more like a fifteen-passenger van crammed with thirty people) doesn't leave until it's full. As one of the first passengers, I stuff my backpack between my legs, sweat dripping down my face, leaving a red mark of dust on my cheek, and I wait. I keep waiting as I watch the sun begin to set. The van is not full, so we are not yet leaving and I am not heading toward home. In my hand I hold a piece of dust-covered paper scribbled with the name of a border town and a family friend I am to meet to spend the final night before going back to my village.

The tears start to come as the hours tick by and I feel my heart beating faster. Worries play out about not having a place to stay or being able to communicate where I need to go. Finally, with the slam of the front door, the driver announces, "Acha, we go!" The engine sputters and we lurch forward as the van roars to life. I feel a trickle of hope mixed in with my tears and sweat.

Darkness descends, and I keep repeating the name of the town I need to be dropped off in. At every stop, I ask, "Here?" My fellow passengers shake their heads at me. My tears make them uncomfortable as they tell me, "It'll be okay, we are going now." Finally, we stop and I hear "Toubab, toubab," everyone pointing at me (the white person) and telling me this is my stop. The other passengers smile at me and point outside the windows. They are not letting me miss my destination. It's pitch-black outside when I exit the bus with a final greeting of peace.

The town is lit by roaring fires. I clench the sheet of paper between my fingers. I don't know anyone in the village. I almost laugh at my stupidity, thinking I'd be able to find my contact easily. This is a town. This isn't a village. I'm tired and I'm caked in dust. I can't remember the last time I washed. I'm determined to find this woman who knows my family in The Gambia and will provide a place to sleep tonight.

There's a gas station on the side of the road. Two men sit on crates around a fire. I approach them with a greeting, "Peace be with you." We continue to greet one another until my patience gets the better of me and I ask if they know Amie, the woman whose home I want to find. They shake their heads and point to the side of their building. "Here," they say. "Sleep here for the night."

"No," I tell them. "I need to clean up and rest."

They point again. "There, clean up," they urge.

I walk around the building through a small door and see a hose attached to the side of the wall. I grab the hose without hesitation. The cold water trickles at first and then floods over my body. Tipping my head back, the water cascades down my face and red dirt pools on the ground.

After I finish, I thank the two men, then continue down the street.

With water from my hair dripping on my shoulders, I ask anyone I meet about my friend. Time is no longer of importance to me. I have no clue what hour of the night I am out searching in the middle of Senegal. Soon I meet someone who knows my friend. "Yes, yes," they say. "She lives not far from here. Let us take you there."

So, off I go in a horse cart, backpack slung over my shoulder, to this Amie's house, whom I'd never met, but who knows my family, and, in turn, knows me. She and her family welcome me, a stranger in the night, still wet from my shower, with the greeting: *Peace be with you.* For this is the African way of hospitality. It's also the way I'm learning to see the world—brimming with holiness and new starts. Buses that serve as confessionals. Fellow passengers bearing witness to pain and loneliness. Hoses that double as fonts.

You may not be lost far from home, but we all get disoriented in big and small ways. We need friends and strangers to guide us. We have unexpected events and illnesses that change our lives in an instant.

In the blessings that follow may you be reminded of the people and places who have shown you the way. May your eyes be open to the fonts of water pouring into your life, reminding you that you never walk alone. May these words provide reprieve for the seasons that feel like too much and the isolation that comes from uncertainty.

If you're lost—whether for a season or a day—hold tight to the hope of a new dawn.

What I Don't Know

Whether prayers are heard
or if they help me or others or God
if words matter at all
if silence is the prayer of the heart
if the answers I seek can be felt
in the whisper of the wind
a sleeping baby
or from the warmth of a flame.

What I don't know
keeps me up at night
fills journals and conversations
feels like screams and shouts
can be heard as *why* and *how* and *how long, O Lord?*

What I don't know
shapes my prayers into
an ongoing conversation
a willingness to be wrong
a chance to be opened and refined
thinking less of me
and more of God.

What I don't know
continues to be my prayer
to be opened to feeling God's presence
to know that I'm not alone
and the desire to pray
is a prayer itself.

A Blessing for Falling Back

God of all time
this is the season of going back
to rhythms and routines
learning and teaching
faces familiar and new
early mornings and (hopefully) early bedtimes
the practice field and the dance hall
the kitchen table strewn with papers and books.

When the world feels heavy
when the needs of our friends press upon our hearts
when we can't take another headline or phone call
I'm sorry I have to tell you this.
When the diagnosis comes in
and our children struggle to fit in,
remember us Lord
and hold us in Your love.

When it feels like we're falling
failing
lost in the wilderness
or holding on by a thread,
You are with us.

When we fall and stumble
when we doubt and wonder
when we yearn for peace
turn our eyes to You
in the dance of the leaves
dawn of a new day
orange fires of twilight
teachers who see beyond the grades
friends who reach out with a handwritten note.

O God of all seasons,
You are here with us
in the new beginnings
and the false starts
in hopes and dreams
in one foot after another
over and over again
Your words pour into our hearts:
I am here, making all things new.

The Things You Carry

List of items in your bag:
keys
bottle
wipes
Legos
spoons
pencils
hair ties
grocery list
old receipts
extra clothes
cherry Lara bar
Kindle Paperwhite
Cheerios and puffs
shriveled orange peel
forgotten permission slips

List of thoughts running through your head:
tired
hungry
more bills

cold coffee
test results
nap time yet?
so much mail
the dog's hair
should I say *Hi*?
eternal to-do list
yelling too much?
the quick temper
where are the keys?
make the appointment
does God really love me?

In this moment, invite God to hold all you carry, including you.

A Blessing for Waiting in the Dark

This blessing is for you,
the one who feels alone
and tired and unsure
wrestling with doubt and belief
who can't seem to move forward
who feels like they are always behind
who can't pay the bills
who is immobilized by fear.

This blessing is for you,
when you wonder if good will prevail
when you worry that all you know is darkness
when your heart breaks and your tears won't stop.

This blessing joins you in the dark,
to remind you that you are not alone.

This blessing knows that the light shines in the darkness
this blessing knows that God's light is near
this blessing knows that God draws us close
this blessing is with you in the dark
never leaving your side
and will be with you
as dawn breaks.

This blessing is for you,
as you wait and wonder and worry
as you question and cry out
as you claw your way toward hope.

A Blessing for Cancelled Plans

This blessing doesn't want to be the bearer of bad news,
that the plans you had been looking forward to
the ones your kids have been talking about nonstop
the date that's been circled on the calendar,
is now cancelled.

This blessing feels your shoulders slump
and the sigh of disappointment
it's there to hold your child when she asks
why can't we still go?
when the son stomps away in tears yelling
but you promised!
and you hold back your own tears.

This blessing knows
you saved and planned and rearranged your days
your heart needed a break, too,
and this date in the planner
written with markers and exclamation points
kept you going on the long days.

But you're here now
with a reality that can't be changed,
so let out the frustration
shed the tears and throw your fists in the air,
then take a breath.

This blessing is here to show you
that something else can fill the space
see what time and opportunities have opened up.
Maybe the plans don't have to be filled,
but rather experienced as a deep breath
an exhale you didn't know you needed
a moment to not have to rush
time spent at home with a good book
or a family movie night
surrounding yourself with people you love.

May this blessing meet you
in the crux of cancelled plans and dashed hope
and take your hand
to illuminate that right now
can still be a gift.

A Blessing for Living with Illness

This blessing is for the one
wading through sickness
watching your body turn against you
doubling over in pain
lying in bed willing yourself to get up
but knowing you can't
waiting in doctors' offices
and being on hold with insurance companies
feeling the weight of all you're unable to attend
and wondering when the relief will come.

This blessing is for the one who must utter
unthinkable words that bring tears and prayers
swears and heartache and so many questions,
the one with a diagnosis they can't pronounce
a sickness so few have had
a disease that didn't run in your family history
but has found you anyway.

There are words no one wants to hear spoken to them:
cancer, tumor, chemo, inoperable, life-expectancy
and there are silences that can only be met
with God's presence.

Hold this sickness and the unknown
the doctor consultations and scans
the pain and the rashes
the side effects that ravage you
hold it all up to the light,
don't give it the power to take your spirit down.

Don't let the fear consume you
even if that's all you feel
for something else is growing around you, too:
love, determination, and courage
the reminder that you are never alone
and even if you don't feel anything
and you can't work up hope
or your brain keeps spiraling into what else might go wrong,
this blessing is here to remind you of those who are in your corner.

This blessing marches with you through
the hospital corridors and outpatient clinics
it knows your fear and heartache

all the questions and what-ifs,
this blessing hears them all and holds you close.

You cry and rage and sit in shock
you pray *why, why, why?*

This blessing carries the words and hope of others
dropping them in your lap
covering you like a handmade quilt
grabbing your hands in an embrace
speaking to you gently,
Peace be with you.

A Blessing for Those Hurt by the Church

Bless you who once felt safe in church
bless you who believed that all were really welcome
bless you who got caught in the middle of gossip and lies
bless you who heard only words of sin and damnation
bless you who trusted the leadership to honor you.

I know you're hesitant
perhaps a bit afraid
to let your heart open again
to let your spirit trust there can be goodness
when you find yourself at church again.

I can only imagine the walls you've put up
to protect yourself and your loved ones
to keep the tears from falling endlessly
and the anger from boiling.

May this blessing meet you
outside of the church

that once felt safe and welcome
but now is filled with hollow platitudes
and memories of God's Word turned against you,
may you find yourself immersed
in the goodness of God's grace
and not in the crosshairs of petty fights.

For this blessing invites you
to come as you are
with your unseen wounds
with all the stories you're holding
of where you've been let down
how you've been harmed
where others have misjudged
where walls have been put up
and individual lives deemed unworthy.

This blessing makes space for your stories,
and believes you.

This blessing knows that the church
does not speak for God
even though you're wondering
where you can find God's peace
and how God could watch you fall so far away.

This blessing wants you to know
that even if you never set foot in a church again,
you are still God's beloved.

But you're here and so is God
as close as your breath
whispering to you
that no matter where you are

and how long you stay away from church
the church has never been
the only place where God dwells.

So take a breath or two
let the tears fall
and be held as
God weeps with you
and brings you home to God's loving arms.

A Blessing to Stop the Scroll

Hours lost
the minutes compound
one after another
for it's never just one email or text
where we lose ourselves
and can't stop the cycle
of checking and scrolling.

Oh Lord, help us reclaim
our time and our attention.

Help us to put down the phone.

Take away the compulsion to check
one more email
or photo
or count shares and likes.

Help us to stop and plug back into our lives
our 3D life of kids and home
work and play
flesh and blood.

May we be more invested
in the people who see our eyes and smile
the ones we can reach with our voices.

May we linger in the present moment
listening to laughter over a meal
car rides passing farms and fields
the way our children drop their bags after school
and the way conversations emerge while waiting in line.

May we be more invested
in creating memories and relishing in them
than posting a picture and sharing a caption online.

May we turn to books and magazines.
May we listen to the hum of insects and the wind rustling
the leaves.
May we keep looking up and see our world before us.

A Blessing for When There Are No Words

What can we say,
when our words only bring tears?

What can we say,
when our mouths cry out in pain?

What can we say,
when the weight of the world feels overwhelming?

Where can we turn,
when no one seems to be listening?

Where can we turn,
when we're afraid for the days ahead?

Where can we turn,
when the road in front of us seems insurmountable?

Between the tears and the anger
and the frustration and the worry
we turn to You, God,
to give us Your peace
to hold our hands
to calm our fears.

May your words meet us:
Come to me all you who are weary
and we come
to lay down our burdens
to give up our worry
to rest in you
to be filled with Your peace.

Bless the prayers we offer,
the ones we speak out loud
the ones that fall with our tears
the ones that speak in righteous anger
the ones that reside deep within
the ones we cannot even utter.

Give us Your peace,
and lead us into Your goodness.

A Blessing for Information Overload

When we can't stop refreshing the latest headline
when we're numb to atrocities across our streets and world
when it all feels like too much and everything is happening
so fast
when we were never meant to hold this much information
and we want a better world for our children,
take this blessing.

Stir up in our hearts the courage
to keep believing there is good
that divides can be overcome
and we can know one another
through small talk at the grocery store
holding the door for one another
volunteering in a school
and listening first before posting on social media.

Give us the wisdom to know truth from fiction,
guard our hearts from rash judgements.

When we need to turn away from the constant information
overload,
help us to learn the names of those we pass every day,
to send a note to a local librarian and a teacher
to make a homemade meal and bring it to someone in pain.

Encourage our hearts
to pray and worship
read a book
or read with a child.

Help us to commit to praying through the headlines
lifting up the names of those we read about

learning more than just the headline,
but of the lived experiences of those in need.

Empower us to use our voice and heart and tears
to bring the world a little closer to God's peace.

A Blessing for Letting Go of the Weight That's Not Yours to Carry

This blessing is for the one who feels deeply
who wants to help everyone
and listen to the hurts of others
and offers words of comfort
who wants to bring peaceful communication to meetings
and everyone to get along.

This blessing is for the one
who hears the pain of their friends
and wants to be there for them
who picks up pizza and paper plates
who writes notes of solidarity
who loses sleep over arguments overheard
or what could have been said differently.

This blessing is for the one
who needs a break
from carrying the emotions
the pain and anger of others
and needs to let their shoulders relax.

Hear these words spoken over you,
you are worthy of rest
and putting down that which was never yours in the first place,
you have your own anxieties and weight to carry

so loosen your grip
on all the other voices vying for your time
hold tight to the people in your circle
and practice saying *no*
walk away from arguments of others
love the people in your home
and guard your heart.

This one life is yours to live
with your own trials and tribulations
your own joys and delight
and enough worries and wonder to fill a lifetime,
so know that it is enough
to be where you are
loving the people and community in front of you
and releasing all the rest.

A Blessing for When Your Child Is Struggling

This blessing already feels the weight you are carrying
the worry that presses you down
and the deep love you have for your children.

Bless you who receives
calls and notes from school
and sees the slumped shoulders as your child comes
home.

Bless you who knows of the problems
whether difficulty turning in homework
not understanding concepts
bullies who taunt
or friendships that turn toward gossip and hurt.

Bless you who provides a safe space
for your children to express their feelings
to know that there's nothing they can say or do
that will ever make you love them less.

May you encourage your children to trust their voice
equip them to seek out allies
and befriend those who love them.

May you offer compassion,
and a hug to envelop them when tears fall.

May you listen and be slow to offer advice.
May you find others who can listen to you, too.

May you find advocates
to provide support and resources
to know that whatever struggles you face
you are in the good company of others.

May you see your child as God designed them
unique and wonderful
wholly loved and wholly yours.

And when the struggles become too much
may you know that together
is how you find the way forward.

A Blessing for Losing Your Patience

Blessed is the one who plays on repeat the one time today she lost her patience. The time she raised her voice. The time she saw a tremble in her daughter's lip. Blessed is the one who longs to take back the temper, rewind time and begin again with a deep breath, not a yell. Blessed is the one who needs to remember she is more than that one moment. She is love and hope and grace for her children, and for herself. May she take that one moment when she yelled and bring it to the light. May she pile on top all the other times she has shown love and patience. Blessed is the one who is learning each day what it means to forgive and be forgiven. Blessed is the one who puts a new voice over her guilt, the voice of God declaring her good and beloved.

A Blessing for When Everyone Else Seems to Have It All Figured Out

If you're constantly trying to keep up
if the pictures on social media
remind you of all you lack
if you thought you'd be more put together at this age
or have more things figured out by now,
lean in and hear this blessing.

This blessing sees you,
trying to be what others expect
following the narrative that always feels unreachable
striving for the polished wardrobe
and a picture-worthy home.

This blessing knows the illusion of social media
and how your heart feels heavy
with every post and picture
seeing the accolades of others
when you've worked so hard yourself
wishing for a family vacation
when you're living paycheck to paycheck
wanting to give your kids that Pinterest-designed party
in every step feeling further and further behind.

Set the phone down
stop worrying how far ahead others seem
and peer deeply into your own life.

For this blessing knows you're doing what you can
and you are the best person for your family
uniquely designed
for such a time as this
called right where you are.

Look around and see your imperfect life
a table full of papers and artwork displaying
creativity
clothes piled on the couch ready to be put away
with memories of play and time together
dishes in the sink
a bed ready to cradle your body
a life without competition
just being where you are
knowing precisely where you're meant to be.

Remember:
God isn't interested
in a well-planned
curated life.
God is interested
in you.

A Blessing for the Haunted

If you're crying out
in horror and disbelief
if your heart can't take another tragedy
of violence and warfare
of bodies strewn and faces in anguish

you are not alone.

If you're wondering
Why God
How God
How long, O Lord

you are not alone.

If your soul aches for this world
for those whose names are unknown
and stories untold

you are not alone.

For we bless and pray and call out
knowing the world is beautiful and horrible
safe for some and a war zone for others
we toss and turn, pray and plead
Why, God, why.

Our prayers—
Come
Peace
Please
Why

Our prayers, our sighs—
How long
How long
How long

Our conviction—
haunted as we look away
while others cannot.

A Blessing for Remembering a Loved One

Maybe a song comes on the radio
a train barrels through the countryside
or you see a sport coat similar to one he wore,
and all of a sudden
memories flood your senses.

Maybe it's their birthday
or your first Christmas with their seat empty
maybe your child delights in old cars just like he did
and you clasp on to the hope
that their love still lives on.

Maybe you still have her faded cookbook
and flip through the pages
imagining the feasts she cooked.

Maybe as the years go by
the memories feel fuzzy
and you go pockets of time
without thinking of them
and you worry you're forgetting.

This blessing wants you to know
the mystery found in loving those who have died,
that their love is with you
woven throughout your days
as close as the hairs on your head.

In the moments you hear a joke they loved to tell,
their love is with you.

In the meals eaten at their favorite restaurant,
their love is with you.

In sharing pictures of their life with your children,
their love is with you.

The love of others
transcending time and place
is beyond our understanding
but nothing is impossible with God
as God's love binds us together
here and now
in this world
and the world to come.

A Blessing for When the World Is on Fire

The world is on fire
and so are our lives
from the people across the ocean
to the teachers across the hall
no one is immune.

The words on our lips feel like curses
Nothing left to do
Cancer
Losing your hair
There's no more money
We have to make some cuts
Those are the orders.

It's too much
our shoulders can't hold the weight
we're shaking and aching
we were never meant to hold this much
and in such fast ways

so we rage
and make phone calls
we're placed on hold
and check our HSA accounts
we tell friends
and let them hold us and our worries
we whisper the unimaginable
and wonder why?
Why? Why? Why?

God, you hold it all
our anger and the uncertainty
we can't do anything to take the pain away
but we pick up today's work
and small acts of hope and courage
and trust that You are there.

Oh Lord, hear our prayers.

A Blessing for When You Want to Give Up on Humanity

But then the man in the pickup truck
stops in the middle of the road
and lets you cross the street
the barista greets you by name
the car in front of you at the drive-through pays for your meal
children skip down the sidewalk
a baby blows a kiss to you
the woman at church offers to keep your toddler entertained
the stranger holds the door for the family carrying groceries
a friend sends a perfectly-timed meme that brings a fit of laughter

the librarian recommends just the right book for your
reluctant reader
and you walk into your local elementary school
and see teachers and staff pour themselves into each child
knowing them by name
and suddenly you aren't so despondent
because day after day
someone else helps you remember
why we're here
and that we need each other
and with the hands and feet of God
citizens keep picking up litter
and raising money when a fire destroys a home
so together we see the truth
that God isn't finished with us yet.

A Blessing for Long Nights

The nights can be long

for new parents
the terminally ill
the one waiting for an answer
the recently widowed
the hungry child
the lonely teenager
the one fleeing their home
the one weathering the storm
the one waiting for work
the one without hope
the one holding on to anger
the addicted
the homeless
the night-shift worker.

In this night
that seems to go on forever
that leaves us wrestling with the dark
with our demons and failings
with the words we forgot to say
and the words we spoke too harshly
with all those we turned our backs on
and those who have turned their back on us
with the sadness of yesterday
and the uncertainty of tomorrow,
shine your light into our nights.

For this night,
may we have a soft place to put our head.

For this sleeplessness,
may we have gentle dreams.

For this life,
may we trust that dawn will always come.

Keep us turning to You
remembering we are not alone
that in our waking and restlessness
the light continues to shine
and the darkness will be overcome.

Bring us together
remind us we are not alone
teach us to pray
to settle us in the silence
to look toward the light
to know You keep vigil with us.

The nights can be long, Lord,
but so is the vastness
of Your love and presence.

A Blessing for Weathering Storms

If you wake with a pit in your stomach
and see a dark sky, with foreboding clouds
streaked of black and gray
and hear a crack of thunder,
grab hold of your loved one's hand.

If you shudder with every lightning flash
and wish for the wind to stop
and the rain not to pound the windows,
close your eyes and take a deep breath.

If you're weathering storms:
an avalanche of grief
unanswered prayers
flooding emotions
unbearable pain
hours on hold on the phone
and darkness that won't let go,
look to the people around you
the ones offering their presence
not platitudes
the ones who show up
rather than turn away
the ones who open their arms
and welcome you in.

Look toward the storm
turn your gaze to the window

and see the storm coming before you
don't shy away
face the rain
open your hands
welcome nature's power
to teach you.

It's here in the thick of life's storms
that you're given a life raft
an anchor to hold you in faith
to be supported
when you feel like you can't go on
to carry you ashore
and see you to the dawning
of a new day.

Called by Name

My mom had my favorite treats and drinks ready and waiting for me upon returning home from both my time in the Peace Corps and walking the Camino. At the airport, I was met with hugs, but also with cold iced tea and bags of Doritos. And of course, there was also the immediate first stop for a cheeseburger and fries.

My mom knew how much the comforts of home meant after being overseas. She understood that knowing someone else means knowing what they love. She understood the gift of sleeping in your own bed after time away and the familiar scent of candles welcoming you back home. After devouring dark chocolate and stopping at the local bakery for donuts, plus taking an extra-long hot shower, my parents took the time to listen to my stories. To know how I felt so far from home and what it was like being back in the house where I grew up. Not many people really want to hear everything about the trips and adventures we've taken, but my parents did. In their listening, they offered their presence and the gift of knowing me.

It doesn't take returning from a monthlong trip to experience the gift of others knowing us.

Many mornings, as we pull into the elementary school parking lot, the kids and I roll down our windows. Following the line of cars with kids bounding out, backpacks and lunch boxes in hand, we're greeted with music. One day we'll hear Taylor Swift's "Shake It Off," another day Pharrell Williams's "Happy," and the next morning the latest Kidz Bop hit. Thanks to the music and catchy beats, there's a dance party in our car and outside the school to start many of our days.

At the school entrance, we're greeted by a few teachers and the principal. Hands are waving, bodies sway to the beat, and our day begins on a high note. As the kids get out of cars, they reach their hands toward the principal, who is waiting with a high five. It's the same every morning—a smile, a dance, and a greeting. Each child greeted by name.

Good morning, Charlotte.
Good morning, Isaac.

When we start our day at the drop-off line with music and high-fives and each student being known by name, I want to cheer for the teachers and share my gratitude. Many days I am brought to tears hearing the kids, every single one of them, addressed by name.

How good it is to be known.
How holy to be called by name.
How beautiful to find home.

We're all walking through life, facing steps of heartache and joys, milestones, and sacred, ordinary days. What a gift it is to have someone call our name. To be known for all our intricacies and gifts. To see us as God does—loved.

The following blessings were written with the hope that wherever you find yourself, you can see your home with God and with God's people. They show us the joy in living room dance parties and practicing gratitude in our everyday lives. These blessings delight in finding home with the simple joys before us, whether in letter writing or making chocolate chip cookies.

May these blessings remind you how deeply God permeates the spaces we inhabit. When we are with God, we are fully ourselves as God created us.

Upon Returning Home

look up
and out
and around
look for stars
and watch light dance on rocks
listen for the call of the eagle
search for blackberries on a summer morn
linger on the porch
look up words in the dictionary
walk barefoot in the grass
eat dessert first
offer a kind word
reach out
write letters
turn off the phone for an hour
savor a sun-ripened tomato
get lost at the library among books
take an off-the-beaten path
call a friend
send the text message: *thinking of you*
light candles
buy the bouquet
rescue the turtle crossing the street
stand in awe under an oak tree
greet the person in front of you
in a word: *love.*

A Blessing for the Hours

This blessing meets you with the early morning dawn
whispering gently: *come, see what the day holds*
it rubs your sleepy eyes and wraps you in a warm blanket
fills the air with the aroma of sizzling bacon and cinnamon rolls
and settles in your heart with God's peace.

This blessing meets you in the afternoon
with a crispness in the air and dancing shadows on your floor
it tells of to-dos, phone calls, and meetings
and reminds you: *you are loved as is*
it delights in watching you care, work, tend, and listen
and settles in your heart, making space for God's peace.

This blessing meets you with the setting sun
in the lighting of candles and gathering at the table
it hears your sighs and prayers and longings
brings hope for a weary world
and settles in your heart, making space for God's peace.

This blessing meets you in the dark of night
wondering and questioning, doubting and believing
it whispers again: *come and rest, I'm here*
it embraces you just as you are
so settle in, rest, breathe, be still
God's peace is here.

A Blessing for Returning to Your Breath

If you feel your heart begin to race
if you can't stop thinking

about all there is to do
the dishes in the sink
what to cook for dinner
how the kids will have time for their homework
the overdue email to your colleague
signing the field trip permission form
following up with the doctor's office,
this blessing is here
to help you find your breath.

Take a deep breath in
through your nose
close your eyes
inhale God's love
feel your feet on the ground
right now
you just have to be here.

And then, just hold
feeling your chest soften
God's Spirit moving within you
God dwelling in you.

Breathe out
through your mouth
with a sigh
letting go of anything but right now
this moment
and your breath
and God's presence.

Hold again
to the love God has for you
the beauty God sees in your life
just as it is,

breathe in
breathe out
until you remember
the closeness of God.

A Blessing for Entering the World Again

If you're weary of the long days of isolation
if you're uncertain how to move forward
if you're unsure of how to be and who to see
if you're tired and worn out
if you're eager for hugs and handshakes
if you're excited to explore and travel,
this blessing is for you.

May you be gentle with yourself
tread lightly if needed
trust the small movements taken in hope
and lean into the One who walks with you.

May you be gentle with others
take time to listen
offer a posture of compassion
and lean into the One who walks with you.

May you be gentle with your surroundings
celebrate the consistency in the changing of seasons
listen for the sounds of spring's renewal
splash in the river's water
and lean into the One who walks with you.

As you move forward,
may the God of infinite love
and boundless grace

bless you and keep you
now and forever.

A Blessing for Marveling at the Stars

If you're wondering about your place in the world
if you're feeling disconnected from God, others, and
yourself
if you need a moment to breathe
and find quiet away from the noise of your life,
go outside at night
and place yourself under a canopy of stars.

Get away from the light of your home
bask in the glow of starlight
marvel at the immense galaxies above you
make a wish on a shooting star.

May you see yourself in this vast galaxy
one piece of a cosmic miracle
connected to stars light-years away
stardust built into your very being.

May you wonder at the Creator
who formed the planets and stars
and your magnificent body
trusting that though you feel small
you are intertwined in an interconnected world
where your place is valued.

May you see the stars above
and know the same stars shine across the world
connecting you to neighbors near and far
a constellation of people looking up together
bearing witness to one another.

Recipe for Joy

Sit
Laugh
Dig in the dirt
Walk barefoot
Breathe deeply
Lean in for hugs
Forge a new path
Follow your children
Linger on the front porch
Let laughter pave the way
Count a tree's growth rings
Dance to the hum of crickets and frogs
Feel ice cream drip down your chin
Believe everything is an adventure
Lean against the trunk of a tree
Watch the sparkle of fireflies
Eat a homemade casserole
Marvel at ripples of water
Savor cold lemonade
Splash in a pool
Give thanks
Look up
Pray.

A Blessing for Living Room Dance Parties

This blessing whirls and twirls
lifts arms up high
and grabs the hands of everyone nearby.

This blessing turns up the music
and turns down anything other than being present to the moment.

This blessing knows the exhilaration found in rhythm and melody
the beauty in bodies moving to the beat
with no concern for appearances,
this blessing looks at you and says:
Come dance.

May you take time to gather in the living room
with friends and family
and move to the flow of the music.

May you see the joy on your children's faces
when everything else is put aside
and all that matters is this single moment.

May you dance to the beauty of your life
a song created for you
in love and grace.

May the soundtrack of your dance parties
be filled with "Dancing Queen"
"YMCA"
Taylor Swift
and Pentatonix.

If the day has been hard
may dancing be the cure
to turn the day around
shake off the sadness
twist out the frustrations
and jump into delight.

When night comes
and nothing else can be done about the day,
turn up the music
and with socked-feet
messy hair
out of breath cheers,
join the dance.

A Blessing for Gratitude

May gratitude in your life
look like a floor strewn with Legos
scraps of paper and markers across the couch
a comfy chair and your favorite book
a full table set with snacks and food for guests
    to enjoy
and Crocs scattered by the front door.

May gratitude
sound like a chorus of *mine* and *me too*
and *please* and *I love you*
Let me get that for you.
How are you?
We missed you.
We're so glad to see you.

May gratitude
smell like a roast simmering in the crockpot
a maple-scented candle burning
your father's aftershave
and an evening campfire.

May gratitude
feel like the first groggy, sleepy-eyed hug of the morning
tiny fingers wrapped in hands

a handwritten letter to turn over and read
bodies pressed together for storytime
and the splashes of water from a bath.

May gratitude
taste like the hundredth handful of Goldfish
steaming hot chocolate and marshmallows
juice boxes shared with friends
dark chocolate and strawberries
and air-fried corn dogs and fries (again).

May gratitude
wrap its arms around you
hold you tight
and say: *look and see*
this life
this day
is brimming with holy gifts.

A Blessing to Remember Goodness

Help me, God, to speak with goodness
to tell of You and Your beauty
the hope You give for those who feel lost
the forgiveness You offer over and over
the love You share unconditionally.

Help me, God, to speak with goodness
of all that I've seen and heard,
a charcuterie board shared with friends
hours of practice perfecting a volleyball serve
voices joining together in song
finding a four-leaf clover
words offered in prayer.

Help me, God, to speak with goodness
to offer words of hope
to freely say: *I love you*
to never miss a chance to say: *I see you*
and: *please forgive me.*

Help me, God, to speak with goodness
and to remember Your words
that You speak to me—
of being called,
loved
beloved
forgiven.

Help me, God,
to speak with goodness.

A Blessing for Play

When your world consists of grown-up tasks
hard conversations and paying bills
keeping track of pills and health checks
managing workers and spreadsheets
responding to emails and reports,
don't forget the power of play.

Change out of your work clothes
pull your hair back
lace your sneakers
and step outside to find a park,
kick your legs on the swing
take a turn down the slide
and listen to the chorus of cheers,
add your voice to the joy.

Grab some paper, markers, crayons, and glue
scatter newspapers on the table
and create,
splatter paint
trace your hand
make a comic
tell a story
and don't worry about coloring in the lines
add your art to the canvas of your day.

Dump blocks on the floor
create towns and imaginary worlds
build racetracks and watch your cars fly
make funny voices and use accents for your characters
get lost in stories and make believe.

Find a board game or a deck of cards
invite friends over for popcorn and a movie
open your doors and set the table
play cheesy get-to-know-you icebreakers
make up silly songs or sing karaoke
turn the music up and dance.

May your heart know the joy found in play
in letting go of worry about how you look
or how you're supposed to act,
but rather run barefoot through the grass
laugh with your whole body
tumble to the floor with the tickle monster
and create for pleasure.

A Blessing for Finding Common Ground

If the news upsets you
if your social feeds make you question where kindness has gone

if you're tired of walking on eggshells
to not upset your family or friends
if you want a safe place for your children,
you are not alone.

Help us to not forget the humanity behind every comment
and story
collectively, may we ask: *how can we move forward?*

Help us to seek another way
the way of loving our neighbors
knowing their stories
hearing what breaks their hearts and brings them joy
and sharing together
a hope for flourishing.

Bless those who turn their tears
toward reaching out to meet others
bless those who take their anger
to prayer and seeking reconciliation
bless those who believe we have more in common than not
and give us the strength to find that unity.

Remind us you are near, Lord
that your heart breaks for every division
and unkind word
and hatred against others
and help us to trust that
we can always start again
listening before speaking
not rushing to judgments
and seeing Your image in those we meet.

Compel us to turn away from screens
and typing responses with a few clicks

but rather to reach out for a handshake
and a nod of the head
to listen with our whole bodies
holding the door open to the stranger
asking the cashier for her name
recommending favorite books to a friend
writing thank-you notes to teachers in your town
picking up garbage at the park.

Bless our small steps and missteps
the times we welcome
and those times we fail to truly see the people in front of us,
but keep us on this path
where we know we are better together
and that our country
our children
need us to work for the common good.

A Blessing for Rainbows

When the rains have passed
the shock of thunder long gone
and the threat of storms fade,
take a moment to breathe in
the lingering scent of rain.

Grab your sweatshirt
and walk outside
through puddles
see the dark clouds interspersed with light
look up and take in the beauty
red, orange, and yellow streaking the sky
catch a glimpse of green, indigo, and violet
be stunned by the long arch soaring through the sky.

Shout to your friends: *rainbow alert.*

May you never tire of going out in the rain
to look for color and light
searching for beauty
amidst life's storms.

How to Be At Peace

Go to the water
even with encroaching deadlines
dishes to clean and laundry to wash
even when doing nothing feels wasteful
sit without an agenda
only becoming present
to breath, wind, water.

Hear the bullfrog croak
watch the dragonflies
twirl and dance around one another
hear splashes
watch ripples of water
feel the breeze on your face
see trees reflecting on the lake
only needing to be present
to plants, creatures, yourself.

Do not pick up the phone to scroll
not forgetting that the world is on fire
but remembering that it is
and your spirit needs the reminder
of the way of the natural world
where seasons come and go
animals sing their songs

the birds still search for worms
make nests for their eggs
where the sun will rise and set
the days will continue
a new dawn always within reach.

Get up and keep breathing
take one step after another
returning to those deadlines, dishes, and laundry
feel the wind
and trust that this peace
will be enough
to face the day.

A Blessing for Hand-Me-Down Clothing

This blessing wraps itself around your children
in your daughter's favorite blue sweater
and your son's ninja pajamas he wears all day
in the winter boots that have played and jumped in snow
the cleats that have chased soccer balls up and down fields.

This blessing gives thanks for friendship
where stories are tucked in coat pockets
handed down winter after winter
where boxes of clothes are packed and saved
ready to be given away to another friend.

May we delight in seeing our children pass on their clothing
and when we see that favorite dress of ours
worn by the kindergartner down the street
may we be reminded
that it takes a village
for it is not only the clothes

but prayers and love
hard-won lessons and solidarity
wrapped in each blanket
and knitted in every shirt.

As we go through drawers and closets
seeing what fits and where pant legs have grown too short
help us remember
the places and memories we experienced with our children
knowing that we can't keep them little forever
but we can pass on love with every item given away.

In every piece of hand-me-down clothing
may we feel God's love
and God's embrace.

May we treasure the current season
dressed in footed pajamas, sequined shirts, and football jerseys
and know that we are forever clothed in God's presence.

A Blessing for Making Chocolate Chip Cookies

This blessing is for you,
when you're in need of a taste of home.

Grab the well-loved cookbook
crisp pages bent from water drops
sugar stuck in the crevices
and memories of days spent dancing in the kitchen,
feel the flour sift through your hands
snack on a chocolate chip (or two)
as you fold them in and watch the dough form.

Let your mind wander
giving thanks for the warmth of the kitchen
the delight in forming balls of dough
as your hands shape the cookies,
pray for the mouths that will consume the sweetness
the stories that will be shared over cookies and milk.

Let your memories take you back
into past kitchens full of flour-dusted counters
yellow Pyrex bowls and the whirling blender
learning how to measure from your mother
sneaking tastes of raw cookie dough,
being safe and known in your home.

As the cookies bake
and the scent fills your kitchen
settle in with some music
while you wash the dishes,
when the timer rings
grab the oven mitts
and feel the rush of hot air
the scent of home
and love mixed in the bubbling chocolate chips.

This blessing is with you,
ready to savor the cookies
to wrap them and give away
to leave some homemade sweetness for the mailman
or the new family down the street
with every bite this blessing says,
take and eat
goodness is before you.

A Blessing for Movie Nights

This blessing delights in gathering as a family
layered under blankets and stuffies
and bowls of popcorn perched on laps
for a movie night.

When the workweek and school days are long
when you're running back and forth to practices and meetings
when some nights you're passing like ships,
this blessing is here to bring you together.

This blessing turns down the phones,
and keeps them out of sight.

This blessing turns up the movies
so that all other worries and distractions are left behind,
if only for a few hours.

This blessing sings along to Disney classics
and introduces your kids to the classics of your youth:
feeling frightened during a thunderstorm with Maria and the Von Trapp kids singing "My Favorite Things"
making your own burglar traps with Kevin from *Home Alone*
and dreaming of your own sandlot for playing baseball.

This blessing laughs and cries
this blessing gives thanks for shared jokes
and twirling princesses
and buttered fingers.

May this time together
be looked upon with gratitude.

May the love shared and comfort extended
go with you and your family
with the reminder that together is the best place to be.

A Blessing for Letter Writing

Feel the paper in your hand
the blank space waiting to be filled
with stories and updates
and love written by hand.

Bless the letter writers and receivers
that in writing a letter
you can feel your pulse soften
your breath slow
your heart fill with gratitude.

May you offer words with pen and paper
to share the small but holy details of your days.

May you take time to choose the perfect stationery:
the rainbow card for a friend celebrating their new baby
the shades and swirls of gray and blue for the one living
    through sickness
the quirky chickens and hedgehogs for the elementary kid
    down the street.

May you notice the way your hand clutches the pen
how cursive letters shine on the paper.

May you write your prayers
inviting another to offer theirs

holding them together
lifting them to God with every stroke.

May you bring comfort
with simple words
I'm here for you
You're not alone
The world needs you.

May you picture friends and family as you write
having a conversation across time
seeing their faces and the way their eyes light up.

What a gift to see erasures and words struck with a line
through them
for we see the thoughts and sentences worked out
knowing that a real person shared glimpses of their real life.

What a gift to see the swirls of *l* and *s*
to notice how *i* is dotted
and the curves of a signature
each word and sentence a testament to living
a life worthy of being known and shared.

The Same Moon

Shines above
where you are
where you have been
with your family
the friends you met last year
and the ones who have known you since birth.

The same moon
casts its light

over cities and towns
side streets and highways
farmlands and market squares
those working through the night
and those fast asleep
the ones rocking babies
and the ones checking temperatures
and doling out cough medicine
the ones who pray to God
and the ones asking: *are you there, God?*

The same moon
rises across the sky
keeping the traveler company
the empty nester on the first night alone
the student away at college
the medic answering a call
the cashier stocking shelves
the parent reassuring a toddler following a nightmare.

The same moon
and the same God
whispers to you: *I am with you*
the light shining in the darkness.

A Blessing for Loving the World

It's not just stepping outside your front door
but the miracle of putting one foot in front of the other
hearing the crunch of leaves
marveling at the clouds above in their various shapes
feeling the ground beneath you
connecting to the natural world with each step.

It's not just sitting with your neighbor
the one with the other political party's sign in their yard
but opening the door to her and her kids:
Come in, have a seat
watching the kids play as if there are no cares at all
as if the fate of your country was on solid ground
looking eye to eye with your friend
not dwelling on who voted for who
but in the moment coming together
for the love of your children.

It's not just the text messages from friends
but tiny threads of connections
words of comfort sent through the universe
me too
we'll get through this.

It's not just dinner
but communion
seated at the table with rumpled clothes
paint-covered fingers
squirrelly bodies
it's listening deeply and asking: *how was your day*?
learning to see each other as beloved
making room
the reminder that there's enough to go around.

It's not just the quiet of the morning
alone with your thoughts
but words and prayers
pleas and cries
a deep breath as you watch the cat claiming the sliver
of light

pouring through the window
as the new day dawns.

A Blessing for the Outrageous

Give a compliment and expect nothing in return
sit, or lie, in the grass
listen to the whisper of the wind
have full conversations with the finches and doves
sing along with the chorus of frogs at night
bake bread, cookies, and muffins
leave on doorsteps and in cars
say *I love you*
offer forgiveness
make friends with your enemy
turn up the music and dance
eat ice cream for breakfast and dinner
say *yes* over and over again
believe in miracles and answered prayers
trust they are true and right on time.

Afterword

Halfway through my pilgrimage on the Camino, I retreat from the heat of the Spanish sun inside a local café. I'm surrounded by buttery croissants, pictures of vineyards and red poppy flowers, and the smell of deep, rich hot chocolate. The owner, tall and tanned, greets me with the traditional, "Buen Camino!" It's been a long day already, with more miles to cover.

With my hot chocolate and baguette, I find a place to sit and rest my blistered feet.

"How do you find the Camino?" I hear from the shopkeeper.

"It's good. Tiring. Beautiful. Life-changing." I struggle to find the words to describe my experience.

"I've walked the Camino multiple times myself." Ah, I think, he knows. He's a pilgrim, too. "You learn that you don't need much in life, all the money and things we have are just extras. If you can live out of a bag for one month, you can do it for years."

I think about how much I've been carrying in my backpack, but also about all the things I've been carrying in my heart, too. I reflect on how I want to take this experience into my life back home. Can I still be a pilgrim when not walking?

Before leaving he tells me a few of his favorite cities along the Camino. He recalls the blisters that slowed him down, and the fellow pilgrims whom he still corresponds with.

"Thank you for your stories," I tell him as I pack my bag and lace my hiking boots.

"Thank you," he tells me and then offers me a blessing. "Everyone finds their own way. Find yours and make it a good one."

The shopkeeper's words have been with me since that day long ago. His blessing lodged deep within my spirit and guided me through my work as a pastor, becoming a mother, and in all my days since. I've found a way that can only be mine—a way of paying attention, seeing the holiness before me, and taking one step after another. Of continuing to be on a pilgrimage.

Now, dear reader, you get to make your own way with these blessings. You're on your own pilgrimage through life, one step after another. My prayer is that you take these blessings when you need them and make them your own. Write your own words to bless yourself and others. Tuck them in your pocket and repeat them over your children. Offer them to the neighbor across the street and the teachers in the classroom. Cry with them when you grieve and smile when they spark joy in your life. However the words meet you, may they become part of your way in seeing God's presence wherever you go.

As with any pilgrimage, either across the world or across the street, you will encounter challenges and joys, heartache and healing, laughter and tears. But through it all, you walk not alone. The way ahead of you is yours, but I hope you'll be able to see God's presence walking beside you. See the holiness around you, and don't forget to wear your boots.

BENEDICTION

May your life be one of small steps
rooted in putting one foot in front of the other
paying attention to the world before you
and seeing glimpses of holiness all around.

May your yearnings and dreams
show you where your heart belongs
and who is cheering for you along the path.

May your work and prayers
pave a way forward
so that you learn from your mistakes
and listen to companions on the way
all while honoring your body's capabilities.

May you take time to rest and renew
drink lots of water
and be sure to look up at the sky.

May you remember
that even when you're lost
you are never alone.

You are here now
where you are meant to be
where you are called
where God knows you by name.

May you listen
for the still small voice of the Spirit,
and may you know this whisper of the Spirit
and feel it in your bones.

May you run and cheer into the wind
and when you fall
may you know the strength of the ground beneath
you.

And perhaps most importantly
when you feel alone and untethered
may you trust that the One who holds you close
walks beside you and whispers:
You are loved.

ACKNOWLEDGMENTS

In The Gambia it's not uncommon to be walking and yell, "*Jerejef!*" to people working in the fields or gardens. *Jerejef* means thank you. The Gambians never shy away from saying thank you to the people they see working. As I finish writing my second book, I'm yelling *thank you* to so many who have walked beside me and supported me in my writing.

I believe the seeds of this book started during seminary when I took an independent study on Christian Pilgrimage. Dr. Lisa Dahill encouraged me to read and write my way through pilgrimage as I prepared for my walk on the Camino. Thank you, Dr. Dahill, for your teaching, friendship, and faith that continues to inspire me.

Writing has never been lonely thanks to the companionship of my writing group—Erin, Melissa, Fay, and Jessica. For all the drafts shared and encouraging words and texts, thank you.

Thanks to the Coffee + Crumbs team and the ladies of Exhale Creativity for modeling what it is to be a mother-writer, and for providing such hospitable and encouraging spaces to share and grow. It's a joy to be writing and mothering alongside you. I vividly remember the C+C retreat in Colorado where I read a blessing for our time together. Your response and encouragement are what finally convinced me to pursue this book. I'm so grateful for the tears and laughter shared in that living room.

Callie Feyen, you have been along for this journey from the beginning. Thanks for being a champion of the writing life. Thanks to Jenna Brack and Sonya Spillmann for your edits and making these blessings sing.

To my local book club, you know what it means to believe in stories and live the reading life. I look forward to our monthly gatherings and the safe space we've cultivated together.

To my pen pal of over thirty years, Annika, thank you for continuing to believe in the power of writing. Thank you to my friend, Erica, for the tech help, the parenting advice, the words of encouragement, and the joy of cultivating a friendship over the years. To the friends who have walked and talked with me—Meghann, Sophie, Lizette, and Amanda—thanks for being our people.

Trinity McFadden and The Bindery, thank you for believing in this book. Morehouse Publishing, thank you for saying yes. Fiona Hallowell, thank you for making the book stronger and clearer and for your consistent presence as I wrote.

To the people of Cole Camp, thank you for cheering on my writing and supporting my books. Every time you purchase a copy or send my writing to your friends, I'm grateful. To the teachers and staff at Cole Camp Elementary School, thanks for welcoming me into your family. I'm in awe of your commitment to your students and the creativity you share daily.

Maybe the beginning of this book can go all the way back to my mom who was my first companion on walks, who first traveled to Spain with me as a high school senior, and who encouraged me in my dreams to serve in the Peace Corps. Thank you will never be enough.

Stephen, Charlotte, and Isaac, you are my biggest blessings. I love you.

ABOUT THE AUTHOR

Kimberly Knowle-Zeller is a writer, pastor in the Evangelical Lutheran Church in America, and mother of two. Many days you can find her walking around town, tending to the garden, or with a pen and paper. Or a good book and a cup of coffee. She believes in the power of words, unearthing the extraordinary in the ordinary, and encouraging others to follow their passions. She writes on the intersection of faith and parenting, searching for holiness in the ordinary. She is the co-author of *The Beauty of Motherhood: Grace-Filled Devotions for the Early Years*, and a contributor to *You're in Good Company: The Gift of Friendship, Motherhood, and Showing Up* as well as *The Message Women's Devotional Bible*. Her widely acclaimed stories on faith and motherhood have appeared in *The Christian Century*, *Living Lutheran*, *Gather* magazine, *Coffee + Crumbs*, and more. She lives in Cole Camp, Missouri.

kimberlyknowlezeller.substack.com
kimberlyknowlezeller.com
Instagram: @kknowlezeller